FRENCH GCSE REVISION ANSWER BOOK

ENVIRONMENT, HEALTH & CAREER

Imprint: Independently Published
Edited by Dylan Viñales

 THE LANGUAGE GYM

ACKNOWLEDGEMENTS

Our gratitude to Martin Lapworth for his time spent creating online versions of the Sentence Builders contained in this book. These are now available, via subscription, on SentenceBuilders.com. The feedback on the final draft, was instrumental in making some key content decisions and tweaks. Thank you.

Lastly, thanks to all the wonderful, supportive and passionate educators on Twitter who have helped enhance our book with their suggestions and comments, and to the members of the Global Innovative Language Teachers (GILT) Facebook group for their engagement with the Sentence Builders series. We consider ourselves very lucky to have such colleagues to inspire and spur us on.

DEDICATION

For Catrina
- Gianfranco

For Mariana
- Ronan

ABOUT THIS BOOK

Welcome,

If you're reading this, it means you've either bought, or are contemplating buying this book.

Either way, thank you.

As with all Language Gym books, our small team has gone to great efforts to produce a high-quality, affordable, no-frills resource. Feedback from the three international and three UK-based schools on the content of this book has been overwhelmingly positive. As with our previous publications, the evidence shows that the EPI method really does produce excellent results. As full-time teachers who use these resources across all levels they teach, Ronan and Dylan can also vouch for the method first-hand. We know that the care taken throughout the creation process will reflect in the quality of the resource and do hope that you and your students enjoy using it!

This book is meant as a revision resource for GCSE French. It can be used independently by students as well as for teacher-directed classroom practice. It contains 12 units which focus mainly on the following themes: "*Environment, Health and Career*".

Each unit consists of a knowledge organiser recapping the target sentence patterns and lexical items, a series of receptive vocab-building activities; a set of narrow reading texts and activities; a set of translation tasks. The tasks are graded in order to pose an increasingly demanding but manageable cognitive load and challenge and are based on Dr Conti's P.I.P.O. framework:

Pre-reading tasks (activation of prior knowledge and pre-teaching)

In-reading tasks (intensive exploitation of tasks)

Post-reading tasks (consolidation)

Output (pushed-output tasks)

Consistent with Dr Conti's E.P.I. approach, each of the 12 units in the book provide extensive recycling of the target lexical items both within each unit and throughout the book, across all the dimensions of receptive and productive processing, i.e.: orthography (single letters and syllables), lexis (both words and chunks), grammar/syntax (with much emphasis on functional and positional processing), meaning and discourse. The recycling occurs through input-flooding and forced retrieval through a wide range of engaging, tried and tested, classic Conti tasks (more than 20 per unit). These include student favourites such as slalom writing, faulty translation, spot the missing detail, sentence puzzles, etc.

Thanks,

Gianfranco & Ronan

THE LANGUAGE GYM

TABLE OF CONTENTS

Unit 1. Food and eating out

1. Match up

Aujourd'hui – *Today*   Ce matin – *This morning*   Ce soir – *This evening*

J'aimerais acheter – *I would like to buy*   Le fromage – *Cheese*   Très savoureux – *Very tasty*

Je ne supporte pas – *I can't stand*   De la viande – *Meat*   Trop épicé – *Too spicy*

Un verre d'eau – *A glass of water*

2. Gapped translation

a. Nous aimerions **commander** un café   b. Je voudrais **acheter** des frites

c. Pour le **dîner**, je mange un **repas** chaud   d. Ce que j'aime **manger**, c'est le **fromage**

e. Ce dont j'ai **horreur**, ce sont les **boissons** gazeuses   f. Ce que j'aime le **moins**, ce **sont** les **légumes**

3. Positive or Negative?

a. Ce que j'aime le plus, c'est la crème brûlée **P**   b. Ce que je déteste manger, ce sont les fritures **N**

c. Ce que je ne supporte pas, ce sont les légumes **N**   d. Ce que j'adore manger, c'est le fromage **P**

e. Ce que je n'aime pas manger, ce sont les fruits **N**   f. Ma nourriture préférée, c'est la quiche lorraine **P**

g. Mon plat préféré, c'est le canard à l'orange **P**   h. Ce dont j'ai horreur, ce sont les crevettes **N**

i. Ce dont je raffole, c'est le chocolat **P**   j. Ce que je préfère manger, c'est le pain **P**

4. Faulty translation

a. Pour le déjeuner: *For **lunch***   b. Les légumes: ***Vegetables***   c. Ce que j'aime le moins: *What I like the **least***

d. Ma nourriture préférée: *My favourite **food***   e. Assez bon: ***Quite** good*   f. Très nourrissant: ***Very** nutritious*

g. Je bois un verre d'eau: *I drink a glass of **water***   h. Ce dont j'ai horreur: *What I **have a horror of***

i. Les boissons gazeuses: ***Fizzy drinks***   j. Trop salé: *Too **salty***

5. Sentence puzzle

a. Ce que j'adore manger, c'est le pain   b. Ce que j'aime le moins, ce sont les légumes

c. Ce que je n'aime pas manger, ce sont les fritures   d. Car c'est trop gras

e. Ce que je ne supporte pas, ce sont les fruits de mer   f. Je bois du chocolat chaud

g. Je prends un verre d'eau   h. Je choisis un repas chaud   i. Je voudrais boire un café

k. Pour le dîner, je mange du poulet avec du riz   l. Car c'est très sain

6. Translate into English

a. I have a hot meal   b. I would like to buy fruit   c. We would like to eat fish   d. What I love eating is bread

e. For snack, I drink hot chocolate   f. For dinner, I eat a hot meal   g. What I prefer eating is cheese

h. Because it's tasty   i. Because it's very greasy and too sweet

7. Broken sentences

Pour le goûter, je bois **du chocolat chaud**   Pour le petit-déjeuner, **je mange du pain**

À midi, je voudrais **manger de la viande**   Ce que j'aime le plus, **c'est la crème brûlée**

Mon plat préféré, c'est **le bœuf bourguignon**   Car c'est vraiment **sain et délicieux**

J'adore le poulet parce **que c'est si bon**   Ce matin, je **voudrais boire un café**

THE LANGUAGE GYM

8. Gapped translation

a. Ce **soir**   b. Nous voudrions **commander**   c. Du chocolat **chaud**   d. Je **bois** un **verre** d'eau

e. J'**aimerais** manger du pain   f. Un **repas** chaud   g. Des boissons **gazeuses**

9. True or false

a. Le café est une boisson **T**   b. Les légumes sont sains **T**   c. Le pain, c'est nourrissant **T**

d. Le bœuf bourguignon, c'est du poisson **F**   e. Le fromage, c'est très sucré **F**

f. Les fritures, c'est assez gras **T**   g. Les crevettes créoles, c'est épicé **T**

10. Complete with the correct verb

a. Nous voudrions **boire** un café   b. Pour le dîner, je **mange** du poulet avec du riz

c. Nous **aimerions** manger des frites   d. Ce que je **préfère** manger, c'est le poisson

e. Ce que j'**aime** le moins, ce sont les légumes   f. Ce dont je **raffole**, c'est le chocolat

g. Ce que je déteste **manger**, ce sont les fritures   h. Ce dont j'**ai** horreur, ce sont les crevettes créoles

i. Ce que je ne **supporte** pas, ce sont les fruits de mer

11. Translate into French

a. *Prawns*: **Crevettes**   b. *Rather*: **Plutôt**   c. *Outstanding*: **Exquis**   d. *Vegetables*: **Légumes**

e. *Cheese*: **Fromage**   f. *Tasty*: **Savoureux**   g. *Chicken*: **Poulet**   h. *Nutritious*: **Nourrissant**

i. *Fish*: **Poisson**   j. *Morning*: **Matin**   k. *Really*: **Vraiment**   l. *Fried foods*: **Fritures**

12. Choose the correct translation

Ce soir – *This evening*   De la viande – *Meat*   Je bois – *I drink*   Sain – *Healthy*   Savoureux – *Tasty*
Trop gras – *Too greasy*   Nourriture – *Food*   Mon plat préféré – *My favourite dish*
Très sucré – *Very sweet*   Pour le déjeuner – *For lunch*

13. Guided translation

a. Ce que j'aime le plus, c'est le fromage   b. Ma nourriture préférée   c. Je préfère manger un repas chaud

d. Mon plat préféré, c'est la mousse au chocolat   e. Ce dont j'ai horreur, ce sont les fritures

f. Pour le dîner, je mange du poulet avec du riz   g. Je bois un verre d'eau   h. Je voudrais acheter de la viande

14. Translate into French

a. À midi, je voudrais manger de la viande avec des frites

b. Aujourd'hui, je voudrais boire un café en ville et après je voudrais acheter des fruits

c. Pour le déjeuner, en général, je mange du poulet avec du riz et je bois un verre d'eau

d. Ce que j'aime manger, c'est le fromage parce que c'est délicieux

e. Ce que je préfère manger, c'est le poisson car c'est sain et savoureux

f. Pour le petit-déjeuner, je mange du pain et du fromage et je bois un café

g. Pour le dîner, je mange un repas chaud. J'aime manger de la viande et des légumes

h. Pour le goûter, normalement je bois un chocolat chaud ou un café et je mange du pain avec du beurre

i. Ce que j'adore manger, c'est le chocolat car c'est sucré et délicieux

j. Ce que je déteste manger, ce sont les crevettes créoles car c'est très épicé et trop salé

15. Find the French equivalent for the following words/phrases in paragraph 1

a. *Today*: **Aujourd'hui**   b. *To buy*: **Acheter**   c. *Meat*: **Viande**   d. *At the butcher's*: **À la boucherie**

e. *A hot meal*: **Un repas chaud**   f. *Vegetables*: **Des légumes**   g. *I am going to have*: **Je vais prendre**

h. *It's good for health*: **C'est bon pour la santé**

16. Faulty translation – Correct the 8 translation mistakes in the translation of paragraph 2 below

In general, I eat **a lot** for breakfast. I have **two** slices of toast with **jam**, butter or honey and I also eat a yogurt with a **banana** and some **cereal**. In addition, I drink a cup of **coffee** and a glass of **fruit** juice. I know that it's very copious, but for me **breakfast** is the most important meal of the day.

17. Complete the sentences below based on paragraph 3

a. What I love is **cheese** because it's **very tasty** and **healthy** so long as we eat it with **moderation**.

b. What I also love eating is **bread** because I **find** this **nutritious**.

c. My favourite **dish** is beef bourguignon because it's **really outstanding** and my mother **cooks** it to **perfection**.

d. My **favourite** dessert is crème brûlée because it's so **good**!

18. Translate into English the following items from paragraph 4

a. Par contre: ***On the other hand***   b. Ce que déteste manger: ***What I hate eating***

c. Ça sent mauvais: ***It smells bad***   d. Ce que je ne supporte pas: ***What I can't stand***

e. Je suis aussi allergique aux noix: ***I am allergic to nuts***   f. Cela me rend malade: ***It makes me sick***

g. Je pense que c'est répugnant: ***I think that it's gross***

19. True, False or Not mentioned?

a. Éric is a vegetarian **F**   b. He eats a lot for breakfast **T**   c. He hates cheese **F**

d. His favourite dish is Fish and chips **F**   e. He loves seafood **F**   f. He is allergic to nuts **T**

g. His brother is allergic to seafood **NM**   h. He thinks eating offal is gross **T**

20. Complete the text with the missing verbs choosing from the options below

À midi, je vais **aller** au restaurant, car c'est l'anniversaire de ma sœur et nous **voulons** fêter cela en famille. Je voudrais **commander** des crudités en entrée, car c'**est** léger et sain et ensuite de la viande et des frites comme plat principal *[main dish]* car j'**adore** cela. Pour le dessert, j'**aimerais** manger une mousse au chocolat et comme boisson, je **vais** probablement prendre un coca ou une limonade.

Mon repas préféré, c'est le dîner et normalement je **mange** beaucoup le soir. Souvent, je mange de la viande rouge avec des pommes de terre ou des pâtes à la sauce tomate accompagnées de légumes biologiques du jardin de mon grand-père. Nous **avons** de la chance car ils **sont** toujours frais et garantis sans pesticides, ni engrais chimiques.

21. True or False?

a. Sophie has a sweet tooth **T**   b. Her favourite dessert is crème brûlée **F**   c. She hates chocolate éclairs **F**

d. Every Saturday, she goes to the bakery to buy croissants and fresh bread **F**   e. She likes spicy food **F**

f. She loves seafood because it's salty **F**   g. She hates fried foods as she finds it too greasy **T**

h. She prefers drinking fizzy drinks because she likes the bubbles **F**

3

THE LANGUAGE GYM

22. Match up

Ce que j'adore manger – *What I love eating*   Les sucreries – *Sweets*   C'est mauvais – *It's bad*
Pour la santé – *For health*   C'est si bon – *It's so good*   Je ne peux pas – *I can't*
Je vais acheter – *I am going to buy*   Du pain frais – *Fresh bread*   En revanche – *On the other hand*
Ce dont j'ai horreur – *What I have a horror of*   C'est trop épicé – *It's too spicy*

23. Answer the questions in English

a. What does Sophie love eating? **She loves eating chocolate and sweets**

b. What are her favourite desserts? **Her favourite desserts are chocolate éclairs and macarons**

c. What does she do every Sunday morning? **She goes to the bakery to buy croissants and fresh bread**

d. What is the dish that she finds too spicy? **Creole prawns**

e. What type of food does she find rather salty? **Seafood**

f. Why does she hate fried foods? **Because it's too greasy**

24. Translate into French

a. Je sais que c'est mauvais pour la santé   b. C'est si bon que je ne peux pas résister

c. Tous les dimanches matin   d. C'est trop épicé pour moi   e. Je n'aime pas les fruits de mer

f. Je préfère la nourriture sucrée   g. Je ne supporte pas les boissons gazeuses

25. Translate the paragraph below, using the chunks in the table on the right-hand side

En général, je mange très peu pour le petit-déjeuner. Je prends seulement une tartine de pain grillé avec de la confiture ou du beurre et parfois, je mange aussi une banane. Comme boisson chaude, je bois une tasse de thé avec du sucre et comme boisson froide, je bois un verre de jus d'orange. Je sais que ce n'est pas assez car le petit-déjeuner est le repas le plus important de la journée.

26. Complete with an appropriate word

a. Je voudrais **acheter** de la viande à la boucherie   b. C'est si bon que je ne **peux** pas résister

c. Ce **dont** j'ai horreur, ce sont les crevettes créoles   d. Ce **que** j'adore manger, c'est le chocolat

e. Mon **repas** préféré, c'est le dîner   f. Je n'aime **pas** les fruits de **mer**   g. Je sais que c'est **mauvais** pour la santé

h. Je bois une **tasse** de café et un **verre** de jus de fruits   i. Je préfère la nourriture **sucrée** comme les desserts

j. Je déteste les fritures car à mon avis c'est trop **gras**   k. J'aime les fruits, car c'est riche en **vitamines**

27. Translate the following sentences into French

a. Pour le déjeuner, en général, je mange du poulet avec du riz et je bois un verre d'eau minérale

b. Ce que j'adore manger, c'est le pain car c'est savoureux et sain

c. Ce que je préfère manger, c'est le poisson parce que c'est salé

d. Ce que je n'aime pas manger, ce sont les fritures car c'est trop gras

e. Je ne supporte pas les boissons gazeuses, car à mon avis, c'est trop sucré

f. Je n'aime pas les crevettes créoles parce que c'est trop épicé pour moi

THE LANGUAGE GYM

Unit 2. Healthy/unhealthy living

1. Choose the correct translation

En bonne santé – ***In good health***   D'habitude – ***Usually***   Dormir – ***To sleep***
Sainement – ***Healthily***   J'essaye de – ***I try to***   Les épinards – ***Spinach***
Je crois que – ***I believe that***   Un régime équilibré – ***A balanced diet***
Nourriture biologique – ***Organic food***   Arrêter de fumer – ***To stop smoking***

2. Match up

Les œufs – *Eggs*   **Je bois** – *I drink*   **Je pense que** – *I think that*   **Je devrais éviter** – *I should avoid*
Des produits frais – *Fresh products*   **J'ai l'intention de** – *I intend to*   **Boire de l'alcool** – *To drink alcohol*
Éviter de fumer – *To avoid smoking*   **Améliorer** – *To improve*   **Tous les jours** – *Every day*
Cuisiner moi-même – *To cook myself*   **Je dois arrêter** – *I must stop*

3. Complete with the correct option from the ones provided below

a. Pour avoir de l'énergie, il faut manger **sainement**   b. Il faut **dormir** huit heures par nuit

c. J'**essaye** de faire de l'exercice régulièrement   d. J'ai l'**intention** de manger plus de légumes

e. J'ai une alimentation **saine**   f. Je suis un régime **équilibré**   g. Je **dois** manger moins de sucreries

h. Je devrais **éviter** de fumer

4. Sentence puzzle

a. J'essaye de dormir huit heures par nuit

b. J'aime assez les oranges car c'est riche en vitamines

c. J'ai l'intention de manger moins de sucreries

d. J'ai l'impression que je suis un régime équilibré car je mange de tout

e. Je crois que je suis en bonne forme car je mange de la nourriture biologique

f. Si j'avais plus de temps, je ferais un effort pour cuisiner plus moi-même

5. Translate into English

a. To stay in shape

b. I try to sleep eight hours per night

c. I like eggs, because it's rich in protein

d. In general, I drink a lot of water

e. I eat a lot of fruit and vegetables

f. If I could, I would cook more myself

g. I intend to eat less sweets

h. I should stop drinking alcohol

i. I should also avoid smoking

j. I am going to make an effort to eat more vegetables

k. I am in good shape because I eat of everything

l. I think I have a healthy diet

m. If I had more time, I would cook more often

n. I believe that I follow a balanced diet

6. True or false?

a. Pour être en bonne santé, il faut fumer et boire beaucoup d'alcool tous les jours **F**

b. Pour avoir de l'énergie, il est important de manger sainement et de dormir huit heures par nuit **T**

c. Pour rester en forme, il faut manger peu de fruits et légumes, mais par contre beaucoup de sucreries **F**

d. Pour améliorer ma santé, je dois boire plus de boissons gazeuses car c'est très sain **F**

e. Pour être en meilleure forme, je devrais éviter de fumer **T**

f. Il est important de manger des fruits et des légumes et de boire beaucoup d'eau **T**

THE LANGUAGE GYM

7. Spot and supply the ONE missing word in each sentence

a. Je vais faire un effort pour manger plus **de** fruits et de légumes

b. Pour rester **en** forme, j'essaye de dormir huit heures par nuit

c. Je crois que je suis **un** régime équilibré, car je mange beaucoup de produits frais

d. J'aime **les** œufs car c'est riche en protéines et en minéraux

e. En général, je bois beaucoup **d'**eau pour le déjeuner

8. Anagrams

a. *Healthily*: **Sainement**   b. *To improve*: **Améliorer**   c. *Organic*: **Biologique**   d. *Diet*: **Alimentation**

e. *Balanced*: **Équilibré**   f. *To sleep*: **Dormir**   g. *Vegetables*: **Légumes**   h. *Sweets*: **Sucreries**

i. *To cook*: **Cuisiner**

9. Complete as appropriate

a. Si je **pouvais**, je cuisinerais plus moi-même

b. Je **devrais** arrêter de boire de l'alcool

c. Je vais faire un **effort** pour manger plus de légumes

d. Pour être en meilleure forme, je devrais **arrêter** de fumer

e. J'aime les œufs, car c'est riche en **protéines**

f. Pour avoir de l'énergie, il est important de manger **sainement**

g. Pour rester en forme, j'**essaye** de faire de l'exercice régulièrement

h. J'ai l'**intention** de manger moins de sucreries

i. Si j'**avais** plus de temps, je cuisinerais plus souvent

10. Correct the spelling errors

a. Je pense que: *I think that*   b. Un régime équilibré: *A balanced diet*

c. Pour améliorer ma santé: *To improve my health*   d. Manger sainement: *To eat healthily*

e. Si j'avais plus de temps: *If I had more time*   f. Pour rester en forme: *To stay in shape*

g. Pour être en meilleure forme: *To be in better shape*   h. Boire de l'alcool: *To drink alcohol*

i. Tous les jours: *Every day*   j. Si je pouvais: *If I could*

11. Complete with the missing accents

a. Pour être en bonne santé   b. En général, je bois du thé sucré   c. Pour améliorer ma santé

d. Je suis un régime équilibré   e. Je dois arrêter de fumer   f. Je devrais éviter de boire de l'alcool

g. C'est très mauvais pour toi   h. Je mange des épinards et je bois du café

i. Je mange régulièrement des légumes   j. C'est riche en minéraux et protéines

THE LANGUAGE GYM

12. Complete the words

a. *To improve*: Amé**liorer**   b. *Healthily*: Sai**nement**   c. *Food*: Nou**rriture**   d. *Organic*: Bio**logique**

e. *Regularly*: Régu**lièrement**   f. *Minerals*: Min**éraux**   g. *Products*: **Produits**   h. *Often*: Sou**vent**

i. *Diet*: Ali**mentation**   j. *Balanced*: Équi**libré**

13. Tangled translation

a. Pour être en bonne **santé**, il faut manger **sainement** et **dormir** huit **heures** par **nuit**

b. Je **pense** that je **suis** un régime **équilibré** car je **mange** beaucoup de produits **frais**

c. **Dans** le futur, je vais **faire** un effort pour manger **moins** de **bonbons/sucreries**

d. **À l'avenir**, j'ai l'intention de manger **plus** de **légumes** et de **boire** moins d'**alcool**

e. Je **devrais** aussi **arrêter** de **fumer** car c'est **mauvais** pour la santé

f. Je pense **que** j'ai une **alimentation** saine **car/parce que** je mange de **tout**

g. Si **j'avais** plus de temps, **je cuisinerais** plus **souvent**

h. **Si** je **pouvais**, je cuisinerais plus **moi-même**

14. Translate into French

a. J'ai l'intention de manger moins de bonbons/sucreries et plus de légumes

b. J'aime assez les oranges car c'est riche en vitamines

c. Je crois que je suis en bonne forme car je mange des produits frais tous les jours

d. Pour avoir de l'énergie, j'essaye de dormir huit heures par nuit

e. Si j'avais plus de temps, je ferais un effort pour cuisiner plus moi-même

f. Pour être en meilleure forme, je devrais arrêter de fumer

g. Dans le futur, je vais faire un effort pour manger plus de fruits

h. Si je pouvais, je cuisinerais plus souvent

15. Find the French equivalent for the following in the text

a. Le sommeil est aussi important que l'alimentation   b. Je fais du sport trois fois par semaine

c. Cela me permet d'éliminer le stress   d. Je bois beaucoup d'eau   e. Je suis végétarien depuis trois ans

f. Avant, je mangeais beaucoup de viande et de fritures   g. Depuis que j'ai arrêté   h. J'ai aussi perdu du poids

i. Je me sens mieux dans ma peau maintenant   j. J'ai l'impression que je suis un régime équilibré

k. Je mange de la nourriture biologique   l. Mauvais pour la santé

m. Je mange toujours un peu de restauration rapide   n. Boissons gazeuses   o. Elles contiennent trop de sucre

16. Complete the translation of paragraph 3

From now on, I have the impression that I **follow** a **balanced diet** because I eat **organic** food every **day** and I don't consume frozen dishes like I used to do in the **past**. They are generally full of **salt** and **fats** and therefore **bad** for health. **I must** recognise that I still eat **a bit** of **fast** food from time to time, but it's **very rare**.

THE LANGUAGE GYM

17. Answer the following questions about Christophe's text

a. What does Christophe do to stay in shape? **He tries to eat healthily**

b. What does he say about sleep? **He tries to always sleep eight hours per night**

c. How often does he exercise? **He exercises three times a week**

d. What are the noticeable improvements with his new diet?

-He feels in better shape -He has more energy -He has lost weight -He feels better in his own skin

e. What does "nourriture biologique" means in English? **The English equivalent is "organic food"**

f. How is he going to improve his health in the future?

-He intends to eat less sweets -He is going to make an effort not to drink fizzy drinks

g. What is he going to avoid doing when he goes out with his friends on Saturdays?

He is going to avoid drinking alcohol (1) and smoking (2)

18. Complete the sentences below based on Lucie's text

a. Every week, Lucie trains **twice** with her **football** club

b. As for food, she tries to eat with **moderation**

c. Usually, she **always** drinks a lot of **water**, around **four** litres per **day**

d. She particularly loves **spinach** because it's rich in **vitamins** and **minerals** and **eggs** because they are rich in protein

e. She also likes **meat**, but she **tries** to eat it only **once** or **twice** per **week**

f. To have energy, she drinks **fresh fruit juice** and she tries to **sleep** at least **eight** hours per **night** because otherwise she is **tired** and in a **bad** mood

g. She has the impression that she has a **healthy** diet because she eats **homemade** organic food

h. She loves cooking and she would like to **become** a **famous/well-known** chef one day and **open** her **own** restaurant

i. To improve her **health**, she must **avoid** drinking alcohol and **smoking** when she sees her friends at the weekend

j. She should also **stop** drinking **fizzy** drinks because the make you **put on** weight and contain a lot of **sugar**

19. True, False or Not mentioned?

a. Lucie trains once a week with her basketball club **F**   b. She has a match every weekend **T**

c. She usually drinks coffee for breakfast **NM**   d. She always drinks a lot of water **T**

e. She particularly likes spinach **T**   f. Her brother hates vegetables **NM**

g. She loves cooking **T**   h. She should start smoking to be healthier **F**

20. Verb quiz

a. Je m'entraîne: *I train*   b. J'essaye: *I try*   c. Je bois: *I drink*   d. Je pense que: *I think that*

e. Je mange: *I eat*   f. Dormir: *To sleep*   g. J'aimerais devenir: *I would like to become*   h. Je vois: *I see*

THE LANGUAGE GYM

21. Translate into English

a. To be in good health   b. It's necessary to exercise regularly   c. I train twice a week

d. I think that I do enough sport   e. I always try to eat with moderation   f. Usually, I drink a lot of water

g. I try to sleep at least eight hours per night   h. I am tired   i. I am in a bad mood   j. I have a healthy diet

k. I eat homemade food   l. I prepare the meals for my family   m. I would like to open my own restaurant

n. I should stop drinking fizzy drinks

22. Correct the spelling/grammar errors

a. Je bois beaucoup **d'**eau   b. J'aime aussi **la** viande   c. Je pense **que** je suis un régime équilibré

d. **Je m'**entraîne deux fois par semaine   e. J'ai l'intention de manger moins de sucreries

f. C'est mauvais pour la santé   g. Je dois éviter **de** boire de l'alcool   h. Ils sont riches **en** vitamines

i. Je bois **du** jus de fruits frais   j. Je dois aussi éviter **de** fumer   k. J'essaye **de** manger sainement

23. Gapped translation

a. *Fizzy drinks*: Des boissons **gazeuses**   b. *Less sweets*: Moins de **bonbons/sucreries**

c. *To stop smoking*: **Arrêter** de fumer   d. *To sleep enough*: **Dormir** assez

e. *Organic food*: De la nourriture **biologique**   f. *Homemade*: Fait(e) **maison**

g. *Only once a week*: **Seulement** une fois par semaine   h. *To avoid drinking*: **Éviter** de boire

i. *A balanced diet*: Un régime **équilibré**   j. *From time to time*: De **temps** en **temps**

k. *Twice a week*: Deux fois par **semaine**

24. Translate the following paragraphs into French

Pour être en bonne santé, J'essaye de manger sainement tous les jours. Pour le petit-déjeuner, je mange du pain et deux œufs et je bois un chocolat chaud. De temps en temps, je bois aussi un jus de fruits frais.

Pour le déjeuner, je mange un repas chaud, normalement du poulet et du riz et je bois de l'eau. J'adore le poulet car c'est sain et délicieux.

Pour rester en forme, il est important de faire de l'exercice régulièrement. Personnellement, je m'entraîne deux fois par semaine avec mon club de foot et j'ai aussi un match tous les week-ends.

Pour améliorer ma santé, je devrais éviter de fumer et de boire de l'alcool quand je sors avec mes amis. Dans le futur, j'ai l'intention de manger moins de sucreries et je vais faire un effort pour manger plus de légumes.

Finalement, si j'avais plus de temps, je ferais un effort pour cuisiner plus moi-même car c'est plus sain et généralement plus savoureux. Je devrais aussi essayer de dormir huit heures par nuit pour être moins fatigué(e).

THE LANGUAGE GYM

Unit 3. Young people and fashion

1. Match up

Actuellement – *Currently*   **Des vêtements** – *Clothes*   **De nos jours** – *Nowadays*   **La mode** – *Fashion*
Les bijoux – *Jewellery*   **Un moyen de** – *A means to*   **Les tatouages** – *Tattoos*   **Triste** – *Sad*
Allure – *Look*   **Tendance** – *Trend*   **Porter** – *To wear*

2. Complete with the correct verb

a. La mode peut **encourager** les moqueries   b. Il faut **laisser** les jeunes développer leur propre allure

c. Les vêtements permettent de se **donner** un genre   d. Les accessoires aident à **améliorer** son image

e. La mode peut **mener** à l'exclusion   f. Les vêtements contribuent à **définir** son identité

g. Les tatouages aident à se **démarquer** des autres

h. On doit encourager les jeunes à **expérimenter** avec des styles différents

3. Gapped translation

a. *Clothes **allow** one to display an image*   b. *Accessories **help** to develop one's identity*

c. *Tattoos help to **stand out** from others*   d. *We must encourage **young people** to experiment*

e. *Personally, I love all the latest **trends***   f. *We **must** let young people develop their own look*

4. Broken words

a. Do**mm**age: *Unfortunate*   b. Actue**ll**ement: *Currently*   c. Ce qui est t**ri**ste: *What is sad*

d. Les dernières tend**ances**: *The latest trends*   e. Des vêtements de ma**rque**: *Branded clothes*

f. Beaucoup de j**eunes**: *Lots of young people*   g. M**ener** à l'exclusion: *To lead to exclusion*

h. Le style vesti**mentaire**: *Clothing style*   i. Les ta**touages**: *Tattoos*

j. La plu**part** des adolescents: *Most adolescents*   k. Les bi**joux**: *Jewellery*

5. Some of the English translations below are wrong. Find them and correct them

a. Ce qui est dommage: *What is **unfortunate***   b. J'adore la mode: *I **love** fashion*

c. Mener à l'exclusion: *To lead to **exclusion***   d. Les tendances actuelles: ***Current** trends*

e. Beaucoup de jeunes: ***A lot of** young people*   f. Des vêtements de marque: *Branded clothes* √

g. Porter des bijoux: *To **wear** jewellery*   h. Leur propre allure: *Their own look* √

i. De nos jours: *Nowadays*   j. La plupart des adolescents: *Most adolescents* √

6. Choose the correct option

a. Il faut **laisser** les adolescents développer leur propre allure

b. On **doit** encourager les jeunes à expérimenter avec différents styles

c. L'apparence est une manière de **s'intégrer** dans un groupe

d. Les accessoires **donnent** l'opportunité de se démarquer des autres

e. Personnellement, j'adore les vêtements **de** marque

f. Ce **qui** est dommage, c'est que **la** mode peut encourager les moqueries

g. En **ce** qui me concerne, j'aime particulièrement m'inspirer des influenceurs d'Instagram

h. Le look est un moyen de se faire **remarquer**

i. De **nos** jours, **la** plupart des adolescents s'habillent **pour** impressionner

7. Find the French for the following in activity 6 above

a. *It is necessary*: Il f**aut**   b. *To fit in*: S'i**ntégrer**   c. *We must*: On d**oit**   d. *A means to*: Un m**oyen** de

e. *To stand out*: Se d**émarquer**   f. *Nowadays*: De n**os jours**   g. *Their own look*: Leur **propre allure**

h. *Fashion*: La m**ode**   i. *Clothes*: Des v**êtements**   j. *Young people*: Les j**eunes**

8. Match the words/phrases of similar meaning

Un moyen de – **Une manière de**   Le look – **L'allure**   Influenceur – **Créateur de contenus**
La plupart des – **La majorité des**   On doit – **Nous devons**   Personnellement – **Pour moi**
De nos jours – **En ce moment**   Triste – **Malheureux**   S'habiller – **Mettre ses vêtements**
Les jeunes – **Les adolescents**

9. Sentence puzzle

a. Beaucoup de jeunes portent des vêtements de marque   b. Parfois, la mode peut mener à l'exclusion
c. Les tatouages aident à se donner un genre   d. Les vêtements contribuent à définir son identité
e. Les bijoux aident à se démarquer des autres   f. J'aime particulièrement les dernières tendances
g. On doit laisser les jeunes développer leur propre allure   h. La mode est une manière de se faire remarquer
i. Je dois dire que j'adore m'inspirer des influenceurs   j. Les accessoires aident à définir son identité

10. One of three

Ce qui est triste – ***What is sad***   Actuellement – ***Currently***   De nos jours – ***Nowadays***
Se donner un genre – ***To display an image***   Des vêtements de marque – ***Branded clothes***
Les dernières tendances – ***The latest trends***   La plupart des jeunes – ***Most young people***
Mener à l'exclusion – ***To lead to exclusion***   Améliorer son image – ***To improve one's image***
Il faut – ***It is necessary***

11. Spot and supply the missing word. NOTE: the missing words are usually small (e.g. articles)

a. De nos jours, **la** plupart des jeunes s'intéressent à la mode
b. L'apparence est une manière de **se** faire remarquer
c. En ce qui me concerne, le look est **un** moyen de s'exprimer
d. Le style vestimentaire permet **de** s'intégrer dans un groupe
e. Ce qui est dommage, c'est **que** la mode peut mener à l'exclusion
f. J'aime particulièrement porter des vêtements **de** marque
g. Je dois dire **que** j'adore m'inspirer des influenceurs d'Instagram
h. Les vêtements donnent **l'**opportunité de s'exprimer

12. Translate into French

a. Les tatouages aident à se démarquer des autres   b. Ce qui est dommage
c. On doit laisser les adolescents développer leur propre allure   d. Il faut laisser
e. En ce qui me concerne   f. Je dois dire que j'adore m'inspirer des influenceurs d'Instagram
g. La mode peut encourager les moqueries   h. Beaucoup de jeunes s'habillent pour impressionner

THE LANGUAGE GYM

13. Complete with a suitable word or phrase

a. Actuellement, la **plupart** des adolescents s'**habillent** pour impressionner

b. De **nos** jours, beaucoup de jeunes **portent** des vêtements de **marque**

c. Le style **vestimentaire** est un **moyen** de s'exprimer

d. Les accessoires pemettent d'**améliorer** son image et de **définir** son identité

e. Il faut **laisser** les adolescents **expérimenter** avec différents styles

f. Ce qui **est** dommage, c'est que la **mode** peut **encourager** les moqueries

g. En ce qui me **concerne**, j'**aime** particulièrement toutes les dernières **tendances**

h. On doit encourager les **jeunes** à **développer** leur **propre** allure

i. Personnellement, je dois **dire** que j'adore m'**inspirer** des influenceurs

14. Find the French equivalent for the following in paragraphs 1 and 2

a. *Them*: **Eux**

b. *Especially*: **Surtout**

c. *Their*: **Leur**

d. *Life*: **Vie**

e. *Consumption*: **Consommation**

f. *Today*: **Aujourd'hui**

g. *A means to*: **Un moyen de**

h. *Youth*: **Jeunesse**

i. *Good*: **Bonne**

j. *Trendy*: **Branchés**

k. *To want*: **Vouloir**

l. *Already*: **Déjà**

m. *Expensive*: **Chers**

n. *Tattoos*: **Tatouages**

o. *Belly button*: **Nombril**

p. *Body*: **Corps**

q. *Makeup*: **Maquillage**

r. *Low-rise jeans*: **Jeans à taille basse**

15. Complete the translation of paragraph 3 below

I **think** that it is important **for** adolescents to be **able** to express themselves fully. It's necessary to **let** them experiment **with** different fashion styles so that with **time** they manage to **define** their **own** identity. We **must** encourage **them** to develop their own look so that it reflects at best their **personality**.

16. Faulty translation: correct the mistakes in the translation of paragraph 4 below (7 mistakes)

At the age when the body is transforming, **young** people **often** wear **more** revealing clothes. These close-fitting outfits such as skin-tight **tee-shirts** showing off curves. Thus, clothing fashion is also a way to get yourself noticed. Young people wishing to seduce are going to **use** fashion as a means to catch the eye of others and test **their** ability to **appeal**.

17. Translate into English

a. De nos jours: *Nowadays*

b. Beaucoup de jeunes: *A lot of young people*

c. Eux: *Them*

d. Mais: *But*

e. Surtout: *Especially*

f. Les autres: *Others*

g. Aujourd'hui: *Today*

h. La jeunesse: *The youth*

i. Branché: *Trendy*

j. Des jeans à taille basse: *Low-rise jeans*

k. Maquillage: *Makeup*

l. Pleinement: *Fully*

m. Au mieux: *At best*

n. Moulant: *Skin-tight*

THE LANGUAGE GYM

18. Complete the following sentences from the paragraphs 1, 2 and 3 then translate them into English

a. La **plupart** des adolescents: *Most adolescents*   b. Que je **connais**: *That I know*   c. Un **moyen** de: *A means to*
d. Dans le **passé**: *In the past*   e. Remettre au **goût** du jour: *To bring back into fashion*
f. Les **réseaux** sociaux: *Social media*   g. Créer son **propre** style: *To create your own style*
h. De **même**: *Likewise*   i. Il faut **laisser**: *It's necessary to let*

19. Complete the sentences below based on paragraph 4

a. Unfortunately, **fashion** also has some **negative** sides that we must not **ignore**.
b. What is **sad** is that it can **lead** to exclusion and **encourage** mocking.
c. **Firstly**, not **everyone** can afford **expensive** clothes and accessories, and this can create a **gap** between young people and **give** birth to cliques at **school**.
d. **Secondly**, some adolescents are not **interested** in fashion, **but** they are still victims of peer **pressure** and the **mocking** of people around them because they are not with it.

20. Find in the text the French equivalent for the following

a. *Currently*: **Actuellement**   b. *Clothes*: **Vêtements**   c. *Young people*: **Jeunes**   d. *Decade*: **Décennie**
e. *Trend*: **Tendance**   f. *Recycling*: **Recyclage**   g. *Look*: **Allure**   h. *Firstly*: **Premièrement**
i. *Secondly*: **Deuxièmement**   j. *Pressure*: **Pression**

21. True or False?

a. The people Damien knows favour comfort over style **F**
b. According to him, physical appearance is not important for young people **F**
c. He says that fashion is constantly recycling itself **T**
d. From what he says, fashion only has positive aspects **F**
e. He mentions that fashion can create a gap between adolescents **T**

22. Complete with the options provided

De nos jours, beaucoup de jeunes portent des vêtement de **marque** pour se faire **remarquer** et pour être branchés. La mode est pour **eux** un **moyen** de s'intégrer dans un groupe. Les accessoires et les **bijoux** leur permettent d'améliorer leur image et de **définir** leur identité.

Je **pense** qu'il faut **laisser** les adolescents développer leur propre **allure** et expérimenter avec différents styles. Personnellement, j'aime particulièrement les dernières **tendances** et je dois dire que j'adore m'inspirer des influenceurs **que** je vois sur les **réseaux** sociaux.

23. Tiled translation

Les jeunes adorent généralement la mode. C'est pour eux, un moyen de s'exprimer et de définir leur identité.

Ils aiment particulièrement les vêtements de marque et les baskets branchées. De même, ils utilisent souvent les tatouages, les bijoux ou les accessoires pour se donner un genre ou pour se démarquer des autres en créant leur propre style.

Malheureusement, la mode a aussi des côtés négatifs et peut parfois encourager les moqueries et mener à l'exclusion.

Certains adolescents ne peuvent pas s'offrir des vêtements chers et cela peut créer un fossé entre jeunes et donner naissance à des cliques au collège.

THE LANGUAGE GYM

24. Split phrases: form logical sentences joining bits from each column

La plupart des adolescents	s'intéressent à la mode
La mode est	une manière de s'exprimer
Il y a un recyclage	des styles anciens
Tout le monde ne peut pas s'offrir	des vêtements et accessoires chers
Malheureusement, la mode	a aussi des côtés négatifs
Les t-shirts moulants mettent	en valeur les formes
Attirer l'	attention des autres
Être victime	de la pression du groupe
Personnellement, j'aime particulièrement	les dernières tendances

25. Translate into French

a. Le style vestimentaire est une manière de s'exprimer

b. De nos jours, beaucoup de jeunes portent des vêtements de marque et s'habillent pour impressionner

c. Nous devons laisser les adolescents développer leur propre allure

d. Malheureusement, la mode a aussi des côtés négatifs

e. Certains adolescents ne peuvent pas s'offrir des vêtements chers

f. Cela peut créer un fossé entre les jeunes et donner naissance à des cliques au collège/à l'école

g. Personnellement, j'aime particulièrement toutes les dernières tendances

h. Ce qui est dommage, c'est qu'être différent peut parfois mener à l'exclusion

26. Translate the following paragraphs into French

La plupart des jeunes aiment particulièrement la mode et toutes les dernières tendances. C'est pour eux, un moyen de s'exprimer et de définir leur identité.

Généralement, ils portent des vêtements de marque et adorent les baskets branchées. De même, ils ont souvent des tatouages, des bijoux ou des accessoires pour se donner un genre ou pour se démarquer des autres en créant leur propre style.

Ce qui est dommage, c'est que la mode peut encourager les moqueries et mener à l'exclusion. Premièrement, certains adolescents ne peuvent pas s'offrir des vêtements chers pour être à la mode.

Deuxièmement, certains adolescents ne s'intéressent pas à la mode, mais ils sont quand même victimes de la pression du groupe. Malheureusement, cela peut créer un fossé entre jeunes et donner naissance à des cliques au collège.

Unit 4. Environment: global problems

1. Match up

Un défi primordial – *A crucial challenge*   Menacer – *To threaten*   L'effet de serre – *The greenhouse effect*
Surconsommation – *Overconsumption*   Gaspillage – *Waste*   Le niveau de la mer – *The sea level*
Inondation – *Flood*   Paysage – *Landscape*   Pénurie – *Shortage*   Empreinte – *Footprint*
Mettre en danger – *To endanger*

2. Complete the words then translate them into English

a. Nourri**ture**: *Food*   b. Réchauffe**ment**: *Warming*   c. L'effet de se**rre**: *The greenhouse effect*

d. Augmenta**tion**: *Increase*   e. Les zones côti**ères**: *Coastal areas*   f. Pays**age**: *Landscape*

g. La population mond**iale**: *World population*   h. Chaque an**née**: *Each year*   i. Le gaspi**llage**: *Waste*

j. Les inon**dations**: *Floods*

3. Phrase puzzle

a. **La pollution de l'eau**: *Water pollution*   b. **L'augmentation de la population**: *The population increase*

c. **En bord de mer**: *At the seaside*   d. **La fonte des glaces**: *The melting of the ice caps*

e. **La montée du niveau de la mer**: *The sea level rise*   f. **Dans les zones côtières**: *In coastal areas*

g. **Le gaspillage de nourriture**: *Food waste*   h. **La diversité de la faune**: *The diversity of fauna*

i. **La pénurie de denrées alimentaires**: *The shortage of foodstuffs*

j. **Le réchauffement climatique**: *Global warming*

4. Anagrams

a. **Paysage**: *Landscape*   b. **Épuisement**: *Exhaustion*   c. **Catastrophes**: *Disasters*   d. **Inondations**: *Floods*

e. **Réchauffement**: *Warming*   f. **Pénurie**: *Shortage*   g. **Surconsommation**: *Overconsumption*

h. **Augmentation**: *Increase*   i. **Empreinte**: *Footprint*   j. **Disparition**: *Extinction*

5. Gapped translation

a. La disparition d'espèces végétales: *The **extinction** of plant species*

b. L'augmentation de la population: *The population **increase***

c. La perte de la biodiversité: *Biodiversity **loss***

d. La fonte des glaces: *The **melting** of the ice caps*

e. La pollution du sol: ***Soil** pollution*

f. L'espèce humaine: *The human **species***

g. Un défi primordial: *A crucial **challenge***

6. Break the flow (phrases)

a. La température des océans   b. La disparition d'espèces animales   c. La montée du niveau de la mer
d. Le gaspillage de nourriture   e. L'épuisement des ressources   f. L'effet de serre
g. L'augmentation de la population

THE LANGUAGE GYM

7. Complete with the options provided

a. La population mondiale ne **cesse** de s'accroître chaque année

b. La fonte des **glaces** contribue aux **catastrophes** naturelles

c. Le **gaspillage** de nourriture joue un rôle important dans la pénurie de **denrées** alimentaires

d. La montée du niveau de la **mer** provoque des inondations

e. La température des océans n'**arrête** pas d'augmenter

f. Le réchauffement climatique est **accéléré** par l'action humaine

g. L'**espèce** humaine impose de plus en plus sa présence dans le paysage

h. L'augmentation de la population rend de plus en plus visible son **empreinte** sur l'environnement

8. Missing letter challenge

a. Un dé**f**i primordial   b. La f**o**nte des glaces   c. En bord de mer   d. Son **e**mpreinte   e. Un problème univers**e**l

f. Le ni**v**eau de la mer   g. Des **i**nondations   h. L'espèce humaine   i. Le pa**y**sage   j. Le gas**p**illage

k. La **s**urconsommation   l. Les zones c**ô**tières

9. Faulty translation: spot and correct the incorrect English translations below

a. La pollution de l'air devient un défi promordial: *Air pollution is becoming a crucial challenge*

b. L'épuisement des ressources est un problème universel: *The exhaustion of resources is a **universal** problem*

c. L'effet de serre est accéléré par l'action humaine: *The greenhouse effect is **accelerated** by human action*

d. La montée du niveau de la mer provoque des inondations: *The sea level rise causes **floods***

e. La population mondiale n'arrête pas d'augmenter: *The world population doesn't stop **increasing***

f. La température des océans continue de s'accroître: *Ocean temperature keeps **growing***

g. La fonte des glaces provoque des inondations: *The melting of the ice caps **causes** floods*

10. Translate into English

a. *Water pollution*   b. *The extinction of animal species*   c. *The melting of the ice caps*

d. *The diversity of flora*   e. *The sea level rise*   f. *In coastal areas*   g. *The world population*

h. *Each year*   i. *Food waste*   j. *The human species*   k. *The population increase*

l. *The exhaustion of natural resources*   m. *At the seaside*   n. *Biodiversity loss*   o. *The greenhouse effect*

p. *Global warming*   q. *Natural disasters*   r. *Each day*   s. *The landscape*   t. *Its footprint on the environment*

11. Gapped translation

a. La pollution de l'air **devient** un **défi** primordial: *Air pollution is becoming a crucial challenge*

b. La **perte** de la biodiversité **est** un problème **universel**: *Biodiversity loss is a universal problem*

c. La fonte des **glaces** provoque des **inondations**: *The melting of the ice caps causes floods*

d. Le **réchauffement** climatique est **causé** par la pollution: *Global warming is caused by pollution*

e. L'effet de **serre** est accéléré par l'action **humaine**: *The greenhouse effect is accelerated by human action*

f. La population **mondiale** n'arrête pas d'**augmenter**: *The world population doesn't stop increasing*

g. La température des océans **continue** de s'**accroître**: *Ocean temperature keeps growing*

h. La **montée** du **niveau** de la mer contribue aux **catastrophes** naturelles dans les zones **côtières**

The sea level rise contributes to natural disasters in coastal areas

12. Sentence puzzle

a. L'effet de serre est accéléré par l'action humaine

b. La population mondiale n'arrête pas d'augmenter

c. La fonte des glaces provoque des inondations

d. La température des océans continue de s'accroître chaque année

e. L'épuisement des ressources est un problème universel

f. Le gaspillage de nourriture joue un rôle important dans la pénurie de denrées alimentaires

g. La surconsommation a une grande influence sur l'épuisement des ressources naturelles

13. Tangled translation

a. La population **mondiale** n'arrête **pas** d'augmenter **chaque** jour

b. La **fonte** des glaces provoque des **inondations**

c. La montée du **niveau** de la **mer** contribue aux **catastrophes** naturelles

d. La **disparition** d'espèces animales **menace** la diversité de la **faune**

e. L'effet de **serre** est **accéléré** par l'action **humaine**

f. L'**épuisement** des ressources **est** un problème **universel**

g. Le **réchauffement** climatique est causé **par** la pollution

h. L'**augmentation** de la population impose de **plus** en **plus** sa présence **dans** le **paysage**

14. Translate into English

a. The greenhouse effect: **L'effet de serre**   b. Global warming: **Le réchauffement climatique**

c. Shortage: **Pénurie**   d. Food waste: **Gaspillage de nourriture**   e. Overconsumption: **Surconsommation**

f. The human species: **L'espèce humaine**   g. Landscape: **Paysage**   h. Each year: **Chaque année**

i. The melting of the ice caps: **La fonte des glaces**

15. Find the French equivalent in paragraphs 1, 2 and 3

a. Nowadays: **De nos jours**   b. All around the world: **Partout autour du monde**

c. Respiratory diseases: **Maladies respiratoires**   d. Health problems: **Problèmes de santé**

e. Likewise: **De même**   f. The extinction: **La disparition**   g. A bit more: **Un peu plus**

h. We now know: **On sait maintenant**   i. To satisfy his needs: **Satisfaire ses besoins**

j. To improve: **Améliorer**   k. Until now: **Jusqu'ici**

16. Complete the translation of paragraph 3

Another problem to **take** seriously is **overpopulation**: world population doesn't **stop** increasing each **year**. Unfortunately, the human **species** is making **more** and **more** visible its **footprint** on the environment in order to satisfy its **needs** and improve its **life** condition. **Until** now, China is the **only** country in the **world** which has been taking **measures** on this subject with its single **child** policy from 1979 to 2015.

17. Place a tick next to the words below which are contained in paragraph 4 and cross the ones which aren't

a. directly √   e. today √   i. overconsumption √

b. linked to √   f. ~~society~~   j. ~~less~~

c. ~~often~~   g. ~~rarely~~   k. more √

d. ~~but~~   h. iron √   l. ~~sometimes~~

THE LANGUAGE GYM

18. Complete the sentence below based on the text

a. Serious natural disasters take **place** regularly   b. Air pollution generates **respiratory diseases**

c. We **now** know that the **greenhouse** effect is accelerated by human action

d. Satisfy its **needs** and **improve** its life condition   e. Today, we **consume** more than we can **afford**

f. **Non-renewable** resources are under pressure

19. Find in the text above:

a. The opposite of 'artificielles': **Naturelles**   b. A synonym of 'sérieuses': **Graves**

c. An adverb starting with 'p': **Pareillement**   d. The opposite of 'heureusement': **Malheureusement**

e. The word for 'warming': **Réchauffement**   f. The opposite of 'réduire': **Augmenter**

g. An adjective derived from 'climat': **Climatique**

20. Find the French equivalent in paragraphs 1, 2 and 3

a. *Across*: **À travers**   b. *Countries*: **Pays**   c. *Strong*: **Forte**   d. *Water*: **Eau**   e. *Everywhere*: **Partout**

f. *Without clean water*: **Sans eau propre**   g. *Earth*: **Terre**   h. *Chemical fertilisers*: **Engrais chimiques**

i. *Springs*: **Sources**   j. *Intensive farming*: **Élevage intensif**   k. *Rivers and lakes*: **Les rivières et les lacs**

l. *Global warming*: **Le réchauffement climatique**   m. *The melting of the ice caps*: **La fonte des glaces**

n. *Not liable to flooding*: **Non inondables**   o. *Coastal areas*: **Les zones côtières**

21. Answer the questions below based on the text

a. What is the common point between every country in the world according to the text?

Every country has environmental problems, they are becoming more and more frequent and intense

b. Why is access to clean water important? **Because life on Earth is not possible without clean water**

c. What is partly responsible for the pollution of groundwater tables? (2 details)

The use of pesticides and chemical fertilisers for agriculture

d. What is one of the causes of pollution in rivers and lakes? **Intensive farming**

e. What is an alarming sign of the water level rising? **Floods in areas that weren't liable to flooding until now**

f. What is happening on a global scale as a consequence of the water level rise?

The sea is gaining ground on the land, which is reducing habitable zones

g. What's the difference between "Terre" and "terre"?

"Terre" with a capital M means "Earth" and terre in lowercase means "land"

22. Correct the following phrases which have been copied wrongly from the text

a. À **travers** le monde: *Across the world*   b. Sans eau **propre**: *Without clean water*

c. **L'utilisation** de pesticides: *The use of pesticides*   d. Des engrais **chimiques**: *Chemical fertilisers*

e. En partie **responsable**: *Partly responsible*   f. **Glissement** de terrain: *Landslide*

23. Translate into English the following words/phrases from paragraph 4

a. En bord de mer: **At the seaside**   b. Constamment: **Constantly**   c. Avec: **With**   d. Du sable: **Sand**

e. Tous les pays: **Every country**   f. Réduire: **To reduce**   g. Les zones habitables: **Habitable zones**

24. Complete with the options provided

De nos **jours**, des **catastrophes** naturelles de plus en plus **graves** ont **lieu** régulièrement partout autour du **monde**. La pollution de l'**air** devient un **défi** primordial et génère de nombreuses **maladies** respiratoires. De même, l'**épuisement** des ressources est **dorénavant** un problème **universel** auquel nous devons rapidement faire **face**.

THE LANGUAGE GYM

25. Tiled translation

De nos jours, il y a de plus en plus de catastrophes naturelles graves à travers le monde entier.

C'est un phénomène inquiétant car les tempêtes génèrent beaucoup de dégâts sur leur passage.

La température globale n'arrête pas d'augmenter et cause la fonte des glaces.

Cela a un impact sur la montée du niveau de la mer et provoque des inondations et de l'érosion côtière sur le littoral de tous les pays.

La mer gagne constamment du terrain sur la terre, ce qui a pour effet de réduire les zones habitables à l'échelle mondiale.

26. Split phrases: form logical sentences joining bits from each column

L'utilisation d'engrais chimiques	terrain sur la terre
Il y a de plus en plus de	en danger la diversité de la flore
Il y a de moins en moins de	catastrophes naturelles
La mer gagne du	un problème inquiétant
La disparition d'espèces végétales met	est en partie responsable de la pollution de l'eau
La perte de la biodiversité est	en plus sa présence dans le paysage
L'espèce humaine impose de plus	zones habitables

27. Complete with the missing verb

a. La montée du niveau de la mer **contribue** aux catastrophes naturelles sur le littoral

b. La population mondiale n'**arrête** pas d'augmenter chaque année

c. La surconsommation **joue** un rôle important dans l'épuisement des ressources naturelles

d. L'espèce humaine **rend** de plus en plus visible sa présence dans le paysage

e. La fonte des glaces **provoque** des inondations dans les zones côtières

f. La disparition d'espèces animales **menace** la diversité de la faune

g. La pollution du sol **devient** un défi primordial

h. La perte de la biodiversité **met** en danger notre vie sur la terre

28. Translate into French

a. La population mondiale n'arrête pas d'augmenter chaque année

b. La surconsommation joue un rôle important dans l'épuisement des ressources naturelles

c. La perte de la biodiversité est un problème universel et menace la vie sur Terre

d. L'effet de serre est accéléré par la pollution et les activités humaines

e. Le gaspillage de nourriture a une grande influence sur la pénurie de denrées alimentaires

f. La montée du niveau de la mer cause des inondations en bord de mer et est en partie responsable de l'érosion côtière

g. L'utilisation de pesticides et d'engrais chimiques cause la pollution de l'eau

h. De même, l'élevage intensif génère de la pollution pour les rivières et les lacs

29. Translate the following paragraphs into French

De nos jours, la pollution de l'air devient un défi promordial pour tous les pays. Chaque année, elle génère de plus en plus de maladies respiratoires et de problèmes de santé partout dans le monde.

De même, la pollution de l'eau est inquiétante car sans eau propre, il n'y a pas de vie possible sur Terre. L'élevage intensif est en partie responsable pour la pollution des sources, des rivières et des lacs.

L'utilisation de pesticides et d'engrais chimiques l'agriculture cause aussi beaucoup de pollution à la campagne.

Dans les zones côtières, la mer gagne constamment du terrain sur la terre, ce qui a pour effet de réduire les zones habitables à l'échelle mondiale. Par ailleurs, le niveau de la mer cause des inondations graves en bord de mer.

19

THE LANGUAGE GYM

Unit 5. Environment: potential solutions

1. Match up

Éviter – *To avoid*   Pour freiner – *To put the brakes on*   Pour protéger – *To protect*
Des produits durables – *Sustainable products*   Acheter – *To buy*   Il est conseillé de – *It is advised to*
À usage unique – *Single-use*   Interdire – *To forbid*   Le gaspillage – *Waste*   La chasse – *Hunting*
Des arbres – *Trees*   Réutiliser – *To reuse*   Il est mieux de – *It is better to*   Les eaux de pluie – *Rainwater*

2. Choose the correct option

a. **Le comportement**: *The behaviour*   b. **L'eau potable**: *Drinkable water*   c. **Lutter**: *To fight*
d. **La hausse**: *The rise*   e. **Interdire**: *To forbid*   f. **Réutiliser**: *To reuse*   g. **L'arrosage**: *Watering*
h. **Le gâchis**: *The misuse*   i. **Ralentir**: *To slow down*   j. **L'utilisation**: *The use*   k. **La cueillette**: *The picking*
l. **Nous pouvons**: *We can*   m. **Il est mieux de**: *It is better to*

3. Phrase puzzle

a. **Il est conseillé de**: *It is advised to*
b. **Diminuer notre consommation d'eau**: *To diminish our water consumption*
c. **Pour sauver notre planète**: *To save our planet*
d. **Pour éviter les sécheresses**: *To avoid droughts*
e. **Pour réduire le gâchis de ressources**: *To reduce resources misuse*
f. **Acheter des produits durables**: *To buy sustainable products*
g. **Diminuer les activités polluantes**: *To diminish polluting activities*
h. **Recycler les déchets**: *To recycle rubbish*
i. **Les espèces en voie de disparition**: *Endangered species*

4. Anagrams

a. **Arbres**: *Trees*   b. **Déchets**: *Rubbish*   c. **Durable**: *Sustainable*   d. **Interdire**: *To forbid*
e. **Gaspillage**: *Waste*   f. **Chasse**: *Hunting*   g. **Mieux**: *Better*   h. **Conseillé**: *Advised*   i. **Hausse**: *Rise*

5. Gapped translation

a. Pour limiter la surconsommation: *To limit **overconsumption***
b. Pour réduire le gaspillage: *To reduce **waste***
c. Acheter des produits durables: *To buy **sustainable** products*
d. Éviter les produits à usage unique: *To avoid **single-**use products*
e. Pour freiner la déforestation: *To **put the brakes on** deforestation*
f. De l'eau potable: ***Drinkable** water*
g. Récupérer les eaux de pluie: *To collect **rainwater***

6. Break the flow (phrases)

a. Les espèces en voie de disparition   b. Pour protéger les animaux   c. Le comportement des individus
d. Éviter les produits à usage unique   e. La cueillette des espèces rares   f. Il est important de planter des arbres
g. Nous pouvons préserver les forêts

20

 THE LANGUAGE GYM

7. One of three

Il est conseillé de – ***It is advised to***   Pour ralentir – ***To slow down***   Les sécheresses – ***Droughts***
La hausse – ***The rise***   Il est mieux de – ***It is better to***   Des arbres – ***Trees***   Le gâchis – ***The misuse***
L'eau potable – ***Drinkable water***   Pour réduire – ***To reduce***   Nous devons – ***We have to***

8. Spot and supply the missing word. NOTE: the missing words are usually small (e.g. articles)

a. Pour éviter **les** sécheresses   b. La chasse des espèces en voie **de** disparition
c. Limiter **l'**utilisation de l'eau potable   d. Il **est** plus éthique d'acheter des produits durables
e. Pour diminuer **la** déforestation   f. Éviter les produits **à** usage unique   g. Nous pouvons planter **des** arbres
h. Il est essentiel **de** bannir les pesticides   i. Il est recommandé de réutiliser **les** objets

9. Match the words/phrases of similar meaning

Combattre – **Lutter**   Il est essentiel de – **Il est vital de**   Bannir – **Interdire**   Ralentir – **Freiner**
En voie de disparition – **Rare**   Sécheresse – **Pénurie d'eau**   Diminuer – **Réduire**   Mieux – **Préférable**
Préserver – **Protéger**   Déforestation – **Déboisement**

10. Sentence puzzle

a. Pour éviter les sécheresses, il faut diminuer notre consommation d'eau
b. Pour préserver la Terre, nous avons besoin de changer le comportement des individus
c. Pour sauver notre planète, nous devons limiter l'utilisation de l'eau potable
d. Pour protéger les animaux, nous devons interdire la chasse des espèces en voie de disparition
e. Pour réduire le gâchis de ressources, il est plus éthique d'acheter des produits durables

11. Wordsearch: find the French translation of the words below

C	O	M	P	O	R	T	E	M	E	N	T					C	
						D	É	C	H	E	T	S	D			H	
		S	É	C	H	E	R	E	S	S	E			U		A	
R	É	D	U	I	R	E		É	V	I	T	E	R			S	
	I	N	T	E	R	D	I	R	E			H	A	U	S	S	E
G	A	S	P	I	L	L	A	G	E				B			E	
							R	É	U	T	I	L	I	S	E	R
C	O	N	S	O	M	M	A	T	I	O	N			E		

hunting: **chasse**   behaviour: **comportement**   rubbish: **déchets**
sustainable: **durable**   to avoid: **éviter**   waste: **gaspillage**
rise: **hausse**   to forbid: **interdire**   to reduce: **réduire**
to reuse: **réutiliser**   drought: **sécheresse**   consumption: **consommation**

12. Complete with the missing accents and then translate into English

a. Pour éviter les sécheresses   b. Pour protéger l'environnement   c. Il est conseillé de recycler les déchets
d. Il est recommandé de réutiliser les objets   e. Il faut éviter les produits à usage unique
f. Pour réduire le gâchis de ressources   g. Il est impératif de diminuer les activités polluantes
h. Nous devons préserver les forêts   i. Nous avons besoin de récuperer les eaux de pluie

THE LANGUAGE GYM

13. Translate into French

a. Pour sauver notre planète   b. Il faut bannir   c. Acheter des produits durables

d. Nous pouvons planter des arbres   e. Nous devons recycler les déchets   f. Changer le comportement des gens

g. Protéger les animaux   h. La pollution du sol   i. To avoid single-use products

j. To limit the use of drinkable water

14. Definition game: match the words on the left with their definition

Durable	Stable, qui est de nature à durer et qui prend en compte l'avenir de la planète
Eau potable	Substance liquide et naturelle que l'on peut boire sans risque d'être malade
Gaspillage	Perte de ressources ou de nourriture
Chasse	Poursuivre des animaux dans le but de les tuer
Sécheresse	Absence ou insuffisance de pluie pendant une certaine période
Pesticide	Produit chimique qui a pour but d'éliminer les parasites et utilisé pour l'agriculture
Interdire	Action de prohiber quelque chose à quelqu'un
Surconsommation	Action d'acheter des choses de manière excessive
Déforestation	Action de détruire une forêt, déboisement d'un espace forestier

15. Find the French equivalent of the phrases or expressions below in Magalie's text (paragraphs in brackets)

a. *To avoid droughts*: **Éviter les sécheresses**

b. *Our water consumption*: **Notre consommation d'eau**

c. *We need to*: **Nous avons besoin de**

d. *To collect rainwater for watering*: **Récupérer les eaux de pluie pour l'arrosage**

e. *In addition*: **Par ailleurs**   f. *Likewise, to reduce waste*: **De même, pour réduire le gaspillage**

g. *To reuse objects*: **Réutiliser les objets**

h. *To give the stuff we don't want anymore*: **Donner les affaires dont on ne veut plus**

i. *To someone else*: **À quelqu'un d'autre**

j. *Or sell them secondhand*: **Ou les vendre d'occasion**

k. *To encourage organic farming*: **Encourager l'agriculture biologique**

l. *As much as possible*: **Autant que possible**

16. Faulty translation – Correct the 8 translation mistakes in the translation of paragraph 3 on the left

To combat **air** pollution, it is essential to **diminish** polluting activities such as transports using **petrol** products or the **industrial** emissions from factories. To fight against **soil** pollution, it is imperative to **ban** pesticides and **chemical** fertilisers and encourage **organic** farming as much as possible.

17. Complete the sentences below based on paragraph 4

a. Finally, to protect animals, it's necessary to firstly **protect their habitat** and to **put the brakes on** deforestation

b. It's important to **plant trees** and to preserve **existing forests**

c. Afterwards, we have to **ban** the hunting of **endangered** species and punish **poaching**

THE LANGUAGE GYM

18. Complete with the missing vowels

a. **Une œuvre de charité**: *A charity*   b. **L'agriculture biologique**: *Organic farming*

c. **Les engrais chimiques**: *Chemical fertilisers*   d. **Le braconnage**: *Poaching*

e. **Utilisant des produits pétroliers**: *Using oil products*   f. **Vendre d'occasion**: *To sell secondhand*

19. Translate into English the following items from paragraph 4

a. Enfin: ***Finally***   b. Tout d'abord: ***First of all***   c. Leur: ***Their***   d. Ensuite: ***Afterwards***

e. Sanctionner: ***To punish***   f. Sévèrement: ***Severely***

20. Find the French equivalent for the following words in paragraphs 1 and 2

a. *Behaviour*: **Comportement**   b. *To learn*: **Apprendre**   c. *Less*: **Moins**   d. *In order to*: **Afin de**

e. *Our*: **Nos**   f. *Current*: **Actuel**   g. *Consumption*: **Consommation**   h. *Choices*: **Choix**   i. *Better*: **Mieux**

j. *Ethical consumers*: **Consom'acteurs**   k. *That's to say*: **C'est-à-dire**   l. *Demanding*: **Exigeant**

m. *To inquire*: **Se renseigner**   n. *Fair trade*: **Commerce équitable**

21. Complete the translation of paragraph 3 below

One of the recent major issues linked to **global warming** is that of intense heat, these **heat waves** are the cause of more and more **devastating** fires each **year**. The **soil** is very dry in times of **drought**, which favours the spread of **flames**. To put the brakes on the rise of temperatures, it's important to **plant trees** and to **preserve forests**.

22. Answer the following questions on paragraphs 3 and 4

a. What is one of the major issues linked to global warming? Why?
Heat waves are one of the major issues because they are at the origin of devastating fires

b. How can we put the brakes on the rise of temperatures according to the text?
It's important to plant trees and to preserve forests

c. What can we do to slow down the exhaustion of resources?
It's advised to recycle rubbish

d. Why do most French people have two separate bins at home?
One is for recyclable products and the other one for organic waste

23. Guided translation

a. *To reduce resources misuse*: **Pour réduire le gâchis de ressources**

b. *To slow down the rise of temperatures*: **Pour ralentir la hausse des températures**

c. *To diminish our water consumption*: **Diminuer notre consommation d'eau**

d. *We have to severely punish poaching*: **Nous devons sévèrement sanctionner le braconnage**

e. *Heat waves are the cause of fires*: **Les vagues de chaleur sont à l'orignie d'incendies**

24. Complete with the correct option choosing from the options below

Pour lutter contre la **pollution** de l'air, il est essentiel de **diminuer** les activités polluantes telles que les **transports** utilisant des produits pétroliers ou les émissions industrielles des **usines**. Pour lutter contre la pollution du **sol**, il est impératif de bannir les **pesticides** et les engrais **chimiques** et d'encourager l'agriculture **biologique** autant que possible.

Enfin, pour **protéger** les animaux, il faut tout d'abord protéger leur **habitat** et freiner la déforestation. Il est important de planter des **arbres** et de préserver les forêts existantes. Ensuite, nous **devons** interdire la **chasse** des espèces en voie de disparition et sanctionner sévèrement le **braconnage**.

 **THE LANGUAGE GYM**

25. Faulty translation (1 or 2 items per sentence)

a. Nous devons apprendre: We **have to/must** learn
b. La finitude des ressources fossiles: The **finiteness** of fossil resources
c. Favoriser les marques éthiques issues du commerce équitable: To favour **ethical** brands from **fair** trade
d. Le sol est très sec en période de sécheresse: The soil is very **dry** in times of drought
e. Nous avons besoin de limiter l'utilisation de l'eau potable: We **need to** limit the use of **drinkable** water
f. Il est conseillé de recycler les déchets: It is **advised** to recycle objects
g. Il faut encourager l'agriculture biologique: It is necessary to encourage **organic** farming
h. Autant que possible: **As much as** possible
i. On peut donner les affaires dont on ne veut plus: We can **give** the stuff that we don't **want** anymore
j. Heureusement, chaque problème a une solution: **Fortunately,** each problem **has** a solution

26. Translate into English

a. To fight air pollution, it is imperative to reduce industrial emissions

b. To protect animals, we have to ban the hunting of endangered species

c. To save our planet, we need to change people's behaviour

d. To avoid droughts, it's necessary to collect rainwater for watering

e. It is important to plant trees and to preserve existing forests

f. We can give the stuff that we don't want anymore to someone else, to a charity or sell them secondhand on the internet for example

g. Our consumption choices have a direct impact on the environment and it's better to buy sustainable products

h. It's essential to properly find out about what we are buying and of course to favour ethical brands from fair trade as much as possible

27. Translate into French

a. Nous devons consommer moins
b. Le rythme mondial actuel de consommation
c. Nos choix de consommation ont un impact direct sur l'environnement
d. Les vagues de chaleur sont la cause d'incendies chaque année
e. La plupart des villes françaises ont maintenant un système de recyclage en place
f. Il est mieux d'acheter des produits durables issus du commerce équitable
g. Nous avons besoin de changer notre comportement
h. Pour éviter les sécheresses, il est vital de limiter l'utilisation de l'eau potable

28. Translate the following paragraphs into French

Pour lutter contre la pollution de l'air, il est essentiel de réduire les activités polluantes comme les transports utilisant des produits pétroliers et les émissions industrielles des usines. Pour diminuer la pollution du sol, il est impératif d'interdire les pesticides et les engrais chimiques et il faut encourager l'agriculture biologique autant que possible.

Par ailleurs, pour ralentir l'épuisement des ressources, il est conseillé de recycler les déchets. De même, pour réduire le gaspillage, il est recommandé de réutiliser les objets ou nous pouvons/on peut donner les affaires dont on ne veut plus à quelqu'un d'autre. Réduire, réutiliser, recycler! Les trois choses importantes à faire pour sauver notre planète.

29. Complete with an appropriate word

a. Il faut encourager l'agriculture **biologique**
b. Il faut favoriser les **marques** éthiques issues du commerce **équitable**
c. Nos choix de **consommation** ont un impact direct sur l'environnement
d. Pour **sauver** notre planète, nous avons **besoin** de changer le **comportement** des individus
e. Pour **éviter** les sécheresses, il faut récupérer les eaux de **pluie** pour l'**arrosage**
f. Il est important de bien se **renseigner** sur ce que l'on achète

Unit 6. What I study, what I like/dislike and why

1. Match up

J'étudie – *I am studying*   Lycée – *Sixth form*   La chimie – *Chemistry*   Divertissant – *Entertaining*
Cours – *Lesson*   Par contre – *However*   Le dessin – *Art*   C'est trop dur – *It's too hard*   Utile – *Useful*
J'apprends – *I am learning*   Compliqué – *Complicated*   Ce que je déteste – *What I hate*
Ennuyeux – *Boring*   Matière scolaire – *School subject*

2. Phrase puzzle

a. **J'étudie le dessin**: *I am studying art*   b. **J'apprends la chimie**: *I am learning chemistry*
c. **Car c'est très divertissant**: *As it's very entertaining*   d. **Car c'est trop compliqué**: *As it's too complicated*
e. **Parce que c'est trop dur**: *Because it's too hard*   f. **Car c'est très utile**: *As it's very useful*
g. **Car je pense que c'est**: *As I think it's*   h. **Parce que je trouve cela**: *Because I find this*
i. **Ce que je déteste**: *What I hate*   j. **Mon cours préféré**: *My favourite lesson*
k. **J'adore cette matière**: *I love this subject*   l. **Car c'est très ennuyeux**: *As it's very boring*

3. Complete the words then translate them into English

a. Le des**sin**: *Art*   b. Par con**tre**: *However*   c. C'est trop d**ur**: *It's too hard*   d. J'app**rends**: *I am learning*
e. J'étu**die** au ly**cée**: *I am studying in the sixth form*   f. Compli**qué**: *Complicated*   g. Ennu**yeux**: *Boring*
h. Diver**tissant**: *Entertaining*   i. Utile: *Useful*   j. Ce q**ue** je dé**teste**: *What I hate*

4. Faulty translation

a. J'étudie la chimie: *I study **chemistry***   b. C'est trop dur: *It's too **hard***   c. J'aime cette matière: *I **like** this subject*
d. C'est utile: *It's **useful***   e. C'est très ennuyeux: *It's very **boring***   f. Au lycée: *In the sixth form*
g. J'apprends: *I learn*   h. J'adore le dessin: *I love **art***   i. C'est trop compliqué: *It's **too** complicated*

5. Translate into English

a. *I am learning drama*   b. *I am studying chemistry in the sixth for*   c. *I am interested in geography*
d. *I think that it's exciting*   e. *What I have a horror of is homework*   f. *This year, I am studying English*
g. *I love this subject*   h. *My favourite lesson is art*

6. Positive or Negative?

a. …car c'est trop difficile **N**
b. …très enrichissant et plutôt facile **P**
c. …parce que c'est créatif **P**
d. …car c'est inutile dans la vie **N**
e. …car selon moi, c'est relaxant **P**
f. …car c'est très motivant **P**
g. …car c'est à mourir d'ennui **N**
h. …parce que c'est trop dur **N**
i. …car c'est trop compliqué **N**

7. Wordsearch: find the French translation of the words below

				H	I	S	T	O	I	R	E				C	
			É	T	U	D	I	E	R			L			H	M
	I	N	F	O	R	M	A	T	I	Q	U	E	Y		I	A
			A					T					C		M	T
			C			C	O	M	P	L	I	Q	U	É	I	I
			I					L					E		E	È
			L			D	U	R		E		T	R	O	P	R
			E					D	I	F	F	I	C	I	L	E

subject: **matière** complicated: **compliqué** history: **histoire**
difficult: **difficile** useful: **utile** easy: **facile**
sixth form: **lycée** IT: **informatique** to study: **étudier**
chemistry: **chimie** hard: **dur** too: **trop**

8. Broken sentences

C'est vraiment **utile** J'étudie la **chimie** Ce que je **déteste** Cette matière **scolaire**
Je pense **que c'est ennuyeux** Je m'intéresse **au dessin** Car **c'est trop dur** Mon cours **préféré**

9. Gapped translation

a. J'étudie la **chimie**: *I study chemistry* b. J'**apprends** l'histoire: *I am learning history*

c. Je m'intéresse au **dessin**: *I am interested art* d. Mon cours **préféré**: *My favourite lesson*

e. Ce que je **déteste**: *What I hate* f. Car c'est trop **dur**: *As it's too hard*

g. Parce que c'est **ennuyeux**: *Because it's boring* h. Cette matière **scolaire**: *This school subject*

i. Vraiment **utile**: *Really useful*

10. Complete with the correct verb

a. Ce que j'aime **étudier** le plus, c'est l'anglais b. Ce que je n'**aime** pas du tout, c'est l'histoire

c. Ce que je **préfère** étudier, c'est le dessin d. Cette année, je me **concentre** sur la géographie

e. Ce que je ne **supporte** pas, c'est l'informatique f. J'aime ce sujet car je **trouve** cela utile

11. Translate into French

a. *Middle school*: **Collège** b. *To study*: **Étudier** c. *Entertaining*: **Divertissant** d. *Sixth form*: **Lycée**
e. *Homework*: **Devoirs** f. *History*: **Histoire** g. *IT*: **Informatique** h. *Easy*: **Facile** i. *Hard*: **Dur**

12. Slalom writing

a. *I love this school subject*: **J'adore cette matière scolaire**

b. *What I have a horror of is homework*: **Ce dont j'ai horreur, ce sont les devoirs**

c. *Because I find this exciting and useful*: **Parce que je trouve cela passionnant et utile**

d. *As it's too complicated*: **Car c'est trop compliqué**

e. *My favourite lesson is art*: **Mon cours préféré, c'est le dessin**

f. *I think that it's very enriching*: **Je pense que c'est très enrichissant**

g. *In my opinion, it's rather easy*: **À mon avis, c'est plutôt facile**

26

 THE LANGUAGE GYM

13. Guided translation

a. *What I like studying the most*: **Ce que j'aime étudier le plus**

b. *What I don't like at all*: **Ce que je n'aime pas du tout**

c. *As it takes time*: **Car ça prend du temps**

d. *Because it's too hard*: **Parce que c'est trop dur**

e. *As according to me, it's relaxing*: **Car selon moi, c'est relaxant**

f. *What I can't stand is IT*: **Ce que je ne supporte pas, c'est l'informatique**

g. *For now, I am interested in chemistry*: **Pour l'instant, je m'intéresse à la chimie**

h. *This year, I am learning history*: **Cette année, j'apprends l'histoire**

i. *At the moment, I am studying drama*: **En ce moment, j'étudie l'art dramatique**

j. *I love this school subject*: **J'adore cette matière scolaire**

14. Complete with an appropriate word/phrase

a. Ce que j'aime étudier le plus, c'est l'**anglais/allemand/espagnol/art dramatique**

b. Ce que je préfère étudier, c'est le **dessin** parce que c'est créatif

c. Mon cours préféré, c'est la **biologie/géographie** car je pense que c'est intéressant et utile

d. J'aime ce sujet, car à mon avis c'est **passionnant** et **motivant (any positive adjectives acceptable)**

e. Par contre, ce que je n'aime pas ce sont les **mathématiques/sciences/devoirs**

f. Par ailleurs, ce que je n'aime pas du tout c'est l'histoire car c'est trop **compliqué/difficile/dur (any negative adjective acceptable)**

g. Mon cours préféré, c'est l'éducation physique et sportive parce que c'est **actif** et **divertissant**

h. Depuis un an maintenant, **j'apprends/étudie** la chimie au lycée et je trouve cela très **intéressant**

15. Sentence puzzle

a. Cette année, j'apprends l'art dramatique et l'histoire à l'école

b. En ce moment, j'étudie la chimie et la physique au lycée

c. Ce que j'aime étudier le plus, c'est l'anglais car c'est très divertissant

d. Ce que je préfère étudier c'est le dessin car selon moi, c'est relaxant

e. Mon cours préféré, c'est l'éducation physique et sportive parce que je trouve cela passionnant et motivant

f. En revanche, ce que je n'aime pas ce sont les devoirs car ça prend du temps

16. Split sentences: join the two chunks in each column to make logical sentences then translate them

1	2	English translation
À mon avis,	**c'est plutôt facile**	*In my opinion, it's rather easy*
Je n'aime pas les sciences	**car c'est trop compliqué**	*I don't like science as it's too complicated*
Je pense que c'est	**très enrichissant**	*I think that it's very enriching*
J'apprends l'histoire et la	**chimie**	*I am learning history and chemistry*
Je m'intéresse	**à la physique**	*I am interested in physics*
Ce que je n'aime pas du	**tout, c'est l'informatique**	*What I don't like at all is IT*
Ce que je déteste ce	**sont les devoirs**	*What I hate is homework*

 THE LANGUAGE GYM

17. Translate into French

a. Mon cours préféré, c'est le dessin car c'est créatif
b. J'adore cette matière scolaire car je pense que c'est assez intéressant
c. À mon avis, c'est plutôt facile
d. Ce que je déteste ce sont les devoirs car ça prend du temps
e. J'aime la géographie car je trouve cela passionnant et utile
f. Je n'aime pas les sciences car c'est trop compliqué
g. Je m'intéresse à la physique car je pense que c'est très enrichissant
h. Cette année, j'apprends l'histoire et la chimie
i. Ce que je n'aime pas du tout, c'est l'informatique car c'est trop dur

18. Find the French equivalent in paragraph 1 and 2

a. *I am learning*: **J'apprends**   b. *I love this school subject*: **J'adore cette matière scolaire**
c. *Really useful for the future*: **Vraiment utile pour le futur**   d. *I would like to study*: **Je voudrais étudier**
e. *Later*: **Plus tard**   f. *In addition*: **Par ailleurs**   g. *Practical to travel*: **Pratique pour voyager**
h. *To work abroad*: **Travailler à l'étranger**   i. *I would like to maybe become*: **J'aimerais peut-être devenir**

19. Complete the translation of paragraph 3

Conversely, what I hate is maths as it's **too** difficult and I **find** it **boring**. Likewise, what I **don't**
like is homework as it **takes time** and I would **prefer** to do something more enjoyable instead.
Unfortunately, I don't have the **choice** and I have to do it or else I get told off by my **teachers**
and my parents!

20. Find in paragraph 4 the following words and translate them into English (except for c and e)

a. A preposition starting with 'd': **Dessus - *Above***   b. A school subject starting with 'h': **Histoire - *History***
c. A noun that means "opinion" in French: **Avis**   d. An adjective starting with 'i': **Inutile - *Useless***
e. A noun that means "things" in French: **Choses - *Things***   f. A noun starting with 'o': **Ordinateur - *Computer***

21. Circle the correct verb

a. J' étudie / aime / **apprends** la géographie: *I am learning geography*
b. J' aime / **adore** / ai cette matière: *I love this subject*
c. J' **étudie** / aide / aime la physique: *I am studying physics*
d. Je pense / **trouve** / supporte cela passionnant: *I find this exciting*
e. C'est à **mourir** / prendre / vivre d'ennui: *It's boring to death*
f. J'aimerais venir / **devenir** / revenir: *I would like to become*
g. Ce que je ne **supporte** / porte / déteste pas: *What I can't stand*

22. Translate into English

a. Later: ***Plus tard***   b. Maybe: ***Peut-être***   c. Conversely: *À l'inverse*   d. Likewise: ***De même***
e. Enjoyable: ***Agréable***   f. Instead: *À la place*   g. Or else: **Sinon**

23. Find the French for the following in the text:

a. *For a year now*: **Depuis un an maintenant**   b. *I would like to become*: **J'aimerais devenir**
c. *I would like to study*: **Je voudrais étudier**   d. *In two years*: **Dans deux ans**   e. *For now*: **Pour l'instant**
f. *I find this subject*: **Je trouve cette matière**   g. *I think that*: **Je pense que**   h. *In addition*: **Par ailleurs**
i. *Sometimes*: **Parfois**   j. *It's too hard*: **C'est trop dur**
k. *I have a horror of computers*: **J'ai horreur des ordinateurs**   l. *I know that*: **Je sais que**

THE LANGUAGE GYM

24. True, False or Not mentioned?

a. Charlotte is studying in a sixth form college **T**   b. She would like to become a lawyer **F**

c. She would like to study physics at university **T**   d. She has a brother and a sister **NM**

e. She can't stand her art teacher **F**   f. She spends more than two hours per day on her homework **T**

g. She hates maths as it's too hard and quite boring **T**   h. She has a passion for computers and loves IT **F**

i. Her best friend studies biology **NM**   j. Charlotte is bad at biology **T**

25. Answer the following questions about the text above

a. What job would Charlotte like to do later? **She would like to be an engineer**

b. How does she find chemistry? **Very difficult**

c. What are the two adjectives that she uses to describe physics? **Enriching and easy**

d. Apart from physics, what is the other lesson she enjoys and why? **Art because it's relaxing and creative**

e. What does charlotte say about maths? (2 details) **She finds maths too hard and quite boring**

f. What does charlotte mention about IT in the last paragraph? (2 details)
It's too complicated and she hates/has a horror of computers

g. What is the expression that Charlotte uses to describe biology in the last paragraph?
She says it's boring to death

26. Guided translation

a. **Je voudrais étudier cela à l'université**   b. **C'est très pratique pour voyager**

c. **J'aime aussi l'art dramatique**   d. **Alors c'est important pour moi**   e. **Je trouve cela assez intéressant**

f. **Je passe plus de deux heures**   g. **Je suis nul(le) dans cette matière**   h. **En même temps**

i. **Je n'ai pas le choix**   j. **J'aimerais travailler à l'étranger**

27. Translate the following sentences in French

a. Mon cours préféré, c'est la physique car je pense que c'est très enrichissant et intéressant

b. J'adore cette matière scolaire car je pense que c'est plutôt facile et vraiment utile

c. Par contre, ce que je déteste, ce sont les mathématiques car c'est trop difficile

d. Ce que je n'aime pas du tout, ce sont les devoirs car ça prend du temps et c'est ennuyeux

e. J'aime le dessin car je trouve cela relaxant et divertissant

f. Je n'aime pas la chimie car c'est trop compliqué pour moi

g. Je m'intéresse à l'art dramatique car je trouve cela motivant et créatif en même temps

h. En ce moment, j'apprends l'histoire et la géographie au lycée

i. Finalement, ce que je ne supporte pas c'est l'informatique car je déteste les ordinateurs

28. Translate the following paragraphs into French

Je m'appelle Nadine et je suis de Bordeaux dans le sud-ouest de la France. J'ai seize ans et j'habite/je vis avec mes parents et mes deux sœurs. Nous avons une maison à la campagne, pas loin de la ville.

En ce moment, j'étudie la chimie et la physique au lycée. J'apprends aussi la géographie et je trouve cela intéressant et plutôt facile.

Ma matière préférée, c'est la physique car je pense que c'est passionnant. Par ailleurs, j'aime aussi le dessin car c'est relaxant et créatif.

Par contre, ce que je n'aime pas du tout, c'est l'histoire car c'est à mourir d'ennui à mon avis.

Plus tard, je voudrais étudier la physique à l'université parce que c'est important pour devenir ingénieure. J'aimerais aussi étudier les mathématiques car c'est très utile dans la vie.

THE LANGUAGE GYM

Unit 7. My post 16 plans

1. Choose the correct translation

Cette semaine – *This week*   Je veux – *I want*   Je crois que – *I believe that*   Un choix – *A choice*
Je ferai – *I will do*   À l'étranger – *Abroad*   Je me renseigne sur – *I am finding out about*
Je vais choisir – *I am going to choose*   Prendre mon temps – *To take my time*
Je vais étudier – *I am going to study*

2. Match up

Je crois que – *I believe that*   Cette semaine – *This week*   À l'étranger – *Abroad*
Je vais choisir – *I am going to choose*   Prendre mon temps – *To take my time*
Je vais étudier – *I am going to study*   Un choix difficile – *A difficult choice*
Études supérieures – *Further studies*   Un engagement – *A commitment*
Filière générale – *Academic pathway*   Je me renseigne sur – *I am finding out about*   Je veux – *I want*
Aller en première – *To go to Year 12*   Sûrement – *Most likely*

3. Complete with the correct verb from the ones provided below

a. Je crois que je **ferai** un apprentissage   b. Je vais **choisir** la filière générale   c. Je **préfère** prendre mon temps
d. J'aimerais **aller** au lycée   e. C'est un choix difficile   f. Je me **renseigne** sur toutes les options
g. Si je **peux**, je prendrai une année sabbatique   h. Je voudrais **passer** le baccalauréat

4. Translate into English

a. I am going to study Spanish   b. I am going to choose maths   c. I would like to go abroad
d. I prefer to take my time   e. It's a difficult choice   f. For my further studies   g. I love this school subject

5. Break the flow (phrases)

a. Je crois que   b. Je vais choisir   c. C'est un choix difficile   d. Je me renseigne sur
e. Prendre mon temps   f. Je vais étudier   g. Si je peux

6. Wordsearch: find the French translation of the words below

					E	N	G	A	G	E	M	E	N	T				M
		E					D	I	F	F	I	C	I	L	E			I
		N		A	P	P	R	E	N	T	I	S	S	A	G	E		E
		T							L	A	N	G	U	E	S			U
		R		É	T	U	D	E	S		I			C	H	O	I	X
		E									È							
				C	O	I	F	F	E	U	R		C	H	O	I	S	I	R
L	A	I	S	S	E	R	T	O	M	B	E	R						

pathway: **filière**   better: **mieux**   apprenticeship: **apprentissage**
to choose: **choisir**   languages: **langues**   commitment: **engagement**
studies: **études**   to drop: **laisser tomber** hairdresser: **coiffeur**
choice: **choix**   between: **entre**   difficult: **difficile**

THE LANGUAGE GYM

7. Missing letters

a. **Je vais choisir**   b. **Cette semaine**   c. **Je préfère prendre mon temps**   d. **Je crois que**   e. **Je veux**
f. **C'est un choix difficile**   g. **Je me renseigne sur**   h. **Pour mes études supérieures**
i. **J'aimerais aller au lycée à l'étranger**   j. **Donc il vaut mieux**

8. Complete as appropriate

a. L'année prochaine, j'**aimerais** aller au lycée   b. Je voudrais vraiment **passer** le baccalauréat
c. Je crois que je vais **choisir** la filière générale   d. Je ferai un apprentissage pour **devenir/être** plombier
e. Je prendrai une année **sabbatique** à l'étranger   f. Je me **renseigne** sur toutes les options possibles
g. Je vais laisser **tomber** l'art dramatique   h. Il vaut mieux **réfléchir** calmement
i. Je préfère **prendre** mon temps   j. C'est un **engagement** sur le long terme

9. Spot and supply the ONE missing word in each sentence

a. Je crois que je **vais** choisir la filière générale
b. Si je peux, je prendrai une année sabbatique **à** l'étranger
c. Cette semaine, je **me** renseigne sur toutes les options possibles
d. Je ferai un apprentissage **pour** devenir coiffeur
e. C'est une décision importante, alors **je** préfère prendre mon temps
f. Ensuite à l'université, j'ai l'intention **de** perfectionner mon anglais
g. Pour **mes** études supérieures, j'envisage de faire un master de commerce
h. Pour le moment, je cherche des informations **sur** toutes les filières disponibles

10. Sentence puzzle

a. L'année prochaine, j'aimerais beaucoup passer le baccalauréat
b. Si c'est possible, je ferai un apprentissage pour devenir coiffeur
c. Si je peux, je prendrai une année sabbatique en Australie
d. Ensuite, à l'université, je voudrais étudier la chimie
e. C'est une décision importante, alors je préfère prendre mon temps
f. Cette semaine, je cherche des informations sur toutes les filières disponibles

11. Tangled translation

a. Je ne sais pas **encore** ce que **je** vais **étudier**
b. C'est un **choix** difficile, **car** je dois **laisser tomber** les maths ou l'**anglais**
c. Si je **peux**, je **prendrai** une **année sabbatique** à l'étranger
d. Ce n'est pas **facile** de choisir, **alors** je préfère **prendre** mon **temps**
e. L'année **prochaine**, j'aimerais beaucoup **aller** au **lycée**
f. **Ensuite**, à l'université, **j'envisage de** perfectionner **mon** anglais
g. **Si** c'est possible, **je ferai** un apprentissage pour **devenir** maçon
h. **Quand** j'aurai fini mes **études** au collège, je voudrais **passer** le bac
i. **C'est** un **engagement** sur le long terme, donc il vaut **mieux** réfléchir

12. Translate into French

a. **Si je peux**   b. **Je vais choisir**   c. **Je voudrais étudier**   d. **Aller au lycée**   e. **Je ferai**
f. **C'est difficile**   g. **À l'étranger**   h. **Devenir**   i. **Alors je préfère**

 **THE LANGUAGE GYM**

13. Guided translation

a. **Si je peux, je prendrai une année sabbatique**
b. **Si c'est possible, je ferai un apprentissage pour devenir coiffeur**
c. **Ce n'est pas facile de choisir, alors je préfère prendre mon temps**
d. **Quand j'aurai fini mes études au collège, je voudrais aller au lycée**
e. **L'année prochaine, je vais étudier l'anglais et la chimie**
f. **Je pense que je vais choisir la filière générale**

14. Find in the text, the French for the following

a. *When I finish*: **Quand j'aurai fini**   b. *Abroad*: **À l'étranger**   c. *The academic pathway*: **La filière générale**
d. *I have good grades*: **J'ai de bonnes notes**   e. *To perfect*: **Perfectionner**
f. *I am going to spend*: **Je vais peut-être passer**   g. *I don't yet know*: **Je ne sais pas encore**
h. *I am looking for some information*: **Je cherche des informations**   i. *Job openings*: **Débouchés**
j. *I am torn (divided)*: **Je suis partagée entre**   k. *To take my time*: **Prendre mon temps**
l. *Without rushing*: **Sans se précipiter**

15. Complete the translation of paragraph 2

I don't **know** yet what I **am going** to do next year, **but** probably literary **studies** as I **like** very much **foreign** languages and I **hate** scientific **subjects**. This **week**, I am looking for some information on **all** the possible options in order to know what the different **diplomas** offer as **job openings**.

16. Answer the following questions in English

a. Why does Adèle want to study at the sixth form college in her town? (2 details)
Because she wants to be with her friends and take her baccalaureate
b. What type of subjects does she enjoy at school? **She likes foreign languages**
c. What does she intend to study at university?
She intends to do a Masters of International Commerce/Business
d. Where would she like to go for her further studies and why?
She would like to study abroad to perfect her English, maybe in England or Canada

17. True, False or Not mentioned?

a. Adèle currently has good grades **T**   b. She already has her baccalauréat **F**
c. She likes studying foreign languages **T**   d. She studies German at school **NM**
e. She would like to go to university in her town **F**
f. She wants to perfect her Spanish by spending a year or two in Spain or South America **F**
g. She would like to set up her own business **T**

18. Translate into French

a. **Aller au lycée**   b. **Je ne sais pas encore**   c. **Je vais faire**   d. **Je suis partagé(e) entre**
e. **Il vaut mieux prendre mon temps**   f. **Étudier à l'étranger**   g. **J'aimerais monter ma propre entreprise**

19. Find the French equivalent in paragraph 1

a. *Once*: **Une fois**   b. *I would like*: **Je voudrais**   c. *Really*: **Vraiment**   d. *Now*: **Maintenant**
e. *I think that*: **Je pense que**   f. *I am going to take*: **Je vais prendre**   g. *Pathway*: **Filière**
h. *I want to do*: **Je veux faire**   i. *In the future*: **Dans l'avenir**

20. Complete with the correct word with the help of the text

a. **Continuer** mes études: *To carry on with my studies*   b. Aller en **pension**: *To go to a boarding school*

c. Je **veux** faire: *I want to do*   d. Un **métier** manuel: *A manual job*

e. J'ai **toujours** voulu **travailler**: *I've always wanted to work*

f. Je **cherche** des informations: *I'm looking for information*   g. **Pas** facile de **choisir**: *Not easy to choose*

h. Prendre mon **temps**: *To take my time*   i. Demander des **conseils**: *To ask for advice*

j. **Nous** guider dans **nos** choix: *To guide us in our choices*   k. **Trouver** sa **voie**: *To find your path*

l. C'est un **boulot** intéressant: *It's an interesting job*

21. Answer the following questions in English

a. Where does Christian live? **He lives in a small village**

b. Where would he like to carry on with his studies? (2 details)

He would like to go to a boarding school in town

c. What type of pathways is he interested in for his future studies?

He is interested in a technological or a vocational pathway

d. What sort of job would Christian like to do? **He would like to do a manual job**

e. In which sector? **In the construction sector**

f. If he goes to university one day, what type of qualification would he do and why?

He would do a professional degree to become site manager

22. True, False or Not mentioned?

a. Christian lives in a small village **T**   b. He wants to go to a boarding school **T**   c. He wants a job in sales **F**

d. He is going to study maths next year **N**   e. A career adviser is helping him **T**

f. He is going to do a law degree **F**   g. A site manager earns less than a worker **F**

23. Match up

Filière – *Pathway*   Lycée – *Sixth form*   Débouchés – *Job openings*   Un défi – *A challenge*

Il vaut mieux – *It's better*   Conseiller – *Adviser*   Disponible – *Available*   Une licence – *A degree*

24. Complete the French sentences

a. **Passer** le baccalauréat: *To take the baccalaureate*   b. J'ai de bonnes **notes**: *I have good grades*

c. Les langues **étrangères**: *Foreign languages*   d. Je vais **choisir**: *I am going to choose*

e. **Monter** ma propre entreprise: *Set up my own business*   f. Nous **voudrions** créer: *We would like to create*

g. Aller en **pension**: *To go to a boarding school*   h. Un **métier** manuel: *A manual job*

i. Dans le **bâtiment**: *In the building trade*   j. C'est **mieux payé**: *It's better paid*

25. Complete using the options provided below

Je ne sais pas **encore** ce que je vais **étudier** l'année **prochaine**, mais je veux aller au **lycée** dans ma ville. Ensuite, pour mes études **supérieures**, j'ai l'**intention** de faire un master de commerce international et j'aimerais beaucoup aller étudier à l'**étranger** pour perfectionner mon **anglais**. Ainsi, je vais **peut-être** passer un ou deux ans en Angleterre ou au **Canada**.

26. Translate into French

a. **Quand je finis/j'aurai fini mes études**   b. **Je voudrais aller au lycée**

c. **Je vais choisir les langues étrangères**   d. **C'est un choix difficile**   e. **Je veux prendre mon temps**

f. **Je voudrais monter ma propre entreprise**   g. **Je préfère les métiers/boulots manuels**

h. **C'est un métier intéressant**   i. **J'ai de bonnes notes dans toutes mes matières**

j. **Je voudrais travailler à l'étranger**   k. **Je vais passer une année en France**

l. **J'ai l'intention de faire une licence de droit**

 **THE LANGUAGE GYM**

27. Spot and supply the missing word

a. J'ai **de** bonnes notes   b. Je voudrais aller **au** lycée   c. C'est **un** choix difficile

d. Je voudrais travailler **à** l'étranger   e. Je vais chercher un boulot **comme** serveur

f. Si **je** peux, je ferai un apprentissage   g. Je ne sais pas encore **ce** que je vais faire

h. Je prendrai **une** année sabbatique   i. Je pense **que** je vais choisir le dessin

j. Je n'ai aucune idée **de** ce que je veux faire   k. J'aimerais étudier **les** langues étrangères

l. J'ai l'intention **de** faire un master de commerce

28. Complete with an appropriate word

a. Si c'est possible, je ferai un apprentissage pour **devenir** plombier

b. L'année **prochaine**, j'aimerais beaucoup aller au lycée

c. Si je **peux**, je prendrai une année sabbatique à l'**étranger**

d. Je pense que je vais **choisir** l'art dramatique ou le dessin

e. Je ne sais pas **encore** ce que je vais étudier, mais je vais probablement choisir la chimie

f. C'est un choix **difficile** car je suis **partagé(e)** entre l'espagnol et la géographie

g. Après mes examens, je vais **chercher** un boulot comme serveur

h. Cela me **passionne**, parce que c'est agréable et bien payé

i. Je n'ai aucune **idée** de ce que je veux faire

29. Translate into French (sentence level translation)

a. Si je peux, je prendrai une année sabbatique à l'étranger

b. Si c'est possible, je ferai un apprentissage pour devenir maçon

c. L'année prochaine, je vais étudier l'anglais et je vais laisser tomber le dessin

d. Si je peux, je voudrais monter ma propre entreprise

e. Je vais passer un an en France pour perfectionner mon français

f. Je préfère les métiers manuels car c'est plus intéressant selon moi

g. Après mes examens, je vais chercher un boulot comme serveur

h. C'est une decision importante, alors je préfère prendre mon temps

i. Cela me passionne, car c'est agréable et varié

j. Pour mes études supérieures, j'envisage de faire une licence de droit

30. Translate the following paragraphs into French

L'année prochaine, je voudrais aller au lycée dans ma ville pour être avec mes amis. Je voudrais étudier la chimie parce que c'est ma matière préférée et je trouve cela très intéressant.

Je crois que je vais choisir des matières scientifiques et je vais laisser tomber l'anglais et le dessin car je trouve ces deux matières trop difficiles.

Ensuite, si je peux, je prendrai une année sabbatique à l'étranger. Je voudrais passer un an en France pour perfectionner mon français. Je vais chercher un boulot comme serveuse ou dans l'hôtellerie ou la vente pour parler français tous les jours.

Pour mes études supérieures, j'ai l'intention de faire une licence de chimie. Puis, si possible, je voudrais travailler comme ingénieure pour une entreprise pharmaceutique.

Unit 8. What job I would like to do and why

1. Match

Faire carrière – ***To make a career***   Devenir comptable – ***To become an accountant***

Travailler comme artisan – ***To work as a craftsman***   Voyager – ***To travel***

Aider les autres – ***To help others***   Devenir chirurgien – ***To become a surgeon***

Étudier la médecine à la faculté – ***To study medicine at university***   Je rêve – ***I dream***

Je veux – ***I want***   Je préfère – ***I prefer***   Je pourrais – ***I could***

2. Spot and correct the 7 wrong translations

a. Selon moi: *According to me*   b. Je rêve: *I dream*   c. Boulots: ***Jobs***   d. Bureau: ***Office***

e. Ils me disent: *They **tell** me*   f. En plein essor: *Fast-growing*   g. Aujourd'hui: ***Today***

h. Comptable: ***Accountant***   i. Je pourrais: *I could*   j. Devenir: *To become*   k. Travail: ***Work***

3. Sentence puzzle

a. Après mes études, je voudrais travailler comme chirurgien

b. Selon moi, c'est une activité qui est en plein essor en ce moment

c. Mes parents me disent que je devrais faire une carrière dans la vente

d. Quant à moi, je préfère les boulots de bureau

e. Selon mes amis, je devrais travailler comme instructeur de sport

f. Je rêve de cette carrière parce que cela semble varié et bien payé

4. Complete the table

English	Français
According to me	Selon moi
Office jobs	**Les boulots de bureau**
I could	**Je pourrais**
I should work	Je devrais travailler
It seems	Cela semble
Varied and well paid	**Varié et bien payé**
To help others	Aider les autres
To become	Devenir

5. Complete with the correct option

a. Selon **moi**: *According to me*

b. **Devenir** chirurgien: *To become a surgeon*

c. **Faire** carrière: *To make a career*

d. Dans la **vente**: *In sales*

e. Travailler **comme** artisan: *To work as a craftsman*

f. En **plein** essor: *Fast-growing*

g. Mes parents me **disent**: *My parents tell me*

h. Je **rêve** de cette carrière: *I dream of this career*

 THE LANGUAGE GYM

6. Translate into English

a. J'aimerais devenir: *I would like to become*

b. Après mes études: *After my studies*

c. Je rêve de cette carrière: *I dream of this career*

d. Selon mes amis: *According to my friends*

e. Mes parents me disent que: *My parents tell me that*

f. Les boulots de bureau: *Office jobs*

g. J'aime cette profession: *I like this profession*

h. Cela semble varié et bien payé: *It seems varied and well-paid*

i. Je voudrais travailler comme artisan: *I would like to work as a craftsman*

j. J'ai l'intention d'étudier la médecine: *I intend to study medicine*

k. Dans la vente: *In sales*

7. Word hunt

a. A verb (infinitive): **Devenir**   b. A job: **Comptable**   c. French for 'job': **Boulot**   d. A subject: **Médecine**

e. A workplace: **Bureau**   f. Another way to say 'in my opinion': **Selon moi**

g. Another way to say university: **Faculté**   h. Opposite of 'avant': **Après**

i. A verb (infinitive): **Faire**   j. A type of job: **Artisan**

8. Wordsearch: find the French translation of the words below

				B	O	U	L	O	T								E
D	E	V	E	N	I	R				S	E	M	B	L	E		R
			F	A	C	U	L	T	É	T	U	D	E	S			È
C	O	M	P	T	A	B	L	E						E			I
	É	Q	U	I	P	E								L			R
							R	Ê	V	E				O			R
			V	O	Y	A	G	E	R					N			A
							A	P	R	È	S						C

job: **boulot**   after: **après**   it seems: cela **semble**

according to: **selon**   team: **équipe**   I dream: je **rêve**

studies: **études**   career: **carrière**   accountant: **comptable**

university: **faculté**   to travel: **voyager**   to become: **devenir**

9. Complete with the missing vowels

a. **En plein essor**: *Fast-growing*   b. **Comptable**: *Accountant*   c. **Devenir**: *To become*

d. **Carrière**: *Career*   e. **Cela semble**: *It seems*   f. **Bien payé**: *Well-paid*   g. **Boulot de bureau**: *Office job*

10. Split phrases

Une carrière dans **la vente**   Je veux devenir **artisan**   Mes parents me **disent que**   Après **mes études**

Je veux travailler **comme comptable**   Cela semble exigeant, mais **gratifiant**   Je rêve **de cette carrière**

Selon **mes amis**

 **THE LANGUAGE GYM**

11. Gapped English-to-French translation

a. Après mes **études**: *After my studies*   b. Selon **moi**: *According to me*
c. J'aimerais **devenir**: *I would like to become*   d. Je **veux** travailler: *I want to work*
e. Cela **semble** exigeant: *It seems demanding*   f. Je **rêve** de cette carrière: *I dream about this career*
g. Je voudrais **travailler**: *I would like to work*   h. Cela semble **gratifiant**: *It seems rewarding*
i. Les **emplois/boulots/métiers** en plein air: *Outdoor jobs*   j. Les boulots de **bureau**: *Office jobs*

12. Spot and supply the missing words

a. Je préfère les boulots **de** bureau   b. Je voudrais travailler dans **la** vente   c. Je rêve **de** cette carrière
d. Mes parents **me** disent **que** je devrais travailler comme comptable   e. Je préfère les emplois **en** plein air
f. À mon avis, c'est une activité qui **est** lucrative   g. Je voudrais travailler **comme** artisan
h. Quant **à** moi, je préfère les boulots de bureau   i. Cela me permettra **d'**aider les autres

13. Complete with the missing letters

a. Après mes études   b. Je veux travailler   c. Les boulots de bureau   d. Les emplois en plein air
e. Je voudrais travailler   f. J'aimerais devenir artisan   g. Je rêve de cette carrière   h. Mes parents disent que

14. Phrase anagrams

a. **Selon moi**   b. **Je voudrais travailler**   c. **Les boulots de bureau**   d. **J'aimerais devenir**   e. **À mon avis**
f. **Les emplois de plein air**   g. **Je rêve**   h. **Cela me permettra de**

15. Complete with an appropriate word

a. Après mes études j'aimerais **travailler** comme avocat
b. Mes parents me **disent** que je devrais travailler dans la vente
c. Je rêve de cette **carrière** parce cela semble exigeant, mais gratifiant
d. Je préfère les **emplois/boulots/métiers** de bureau
e. Selon moi, c'est une **industrie/activité** très lucrative
f. Je veux travailler **comme** instructeur de sport
g. Je voudrais **devenir** chirurgien
h. Selon mon frère, je devrais **étudier** la médecine à la faculté
i. **Quant** à moi, je préfère les emplois en plein air
j. Je préfère le **travail** indépendant, alors je veux devenir avocat

16. Guided translation

a. *According to me*: **Selon moi**   b. *Outdoor jobs*: **Les emplois en plein air**   c. *I dream*: **Je rêve**
d. *In my opinion*: **À mon avis**   e. *After my studies*: **Après mes études**   f. *I want to work*: **Je veux travailler**
g. *Office jobs*: **Les boulots de bureau**   h. *I would like to become*: **Je voudrais devenir**
i. *I would like to work*: **Je voudrais travailler**   j. *As a craftsman*: **Comme artisan**
k. *As a surgeon*: **Comme chirurgien**   l. *My parents tell me that*: **Mes parents me disent que**
m. *It seems*: **Cela semble**

17. Find the French equivalent in the text in paragraph 1

a. *I will have*: **J'aurai**   b. *I hope to be*: **J'espère être**   c. *This job*: **Ce métier**
d. *It seems to be*: **Cela semble être**   e. *Not too tiring*: **Pas trop fatigant**
f. *I am passionate about*: **Je suis passionné de**   g. *I would like to help*: **Je voudrais aider**
h. *Which*: **Ce qui**   i. *People*: **Les gens**   j. *Good health*: **Bonne santé**

18. Complete the translation of paragraph 2

My brother **tells** that I could **try** to work as a **scuba diving** instructor and live in the Maldives for **a few** years. I must **admit** that I **love** this sport, but **maybe** not to the extent of making it my **job**. Moreover, if I am a **surgeon**, I will be able to afford some **holidays** to the Maldives, which is **better** than working there **according to** me.

19. Spot and supply the <u>eight</u> missing words in this wrong version of paragraph 3

Moi, je préfère **les** boulots **en** intérieur, alors le métier **de** chirurgien serait parfait. Par ailleurs, j'aime le travail d'équipe et dans **un** hôpital, on **ne** travaille jamais seul. Le secteur medical est également un **des** plus importants, car il a pour but **de** soigner et de protéger **la** vie humaine.

20. Translate into English the words below taken from paragraph 3

a. Boulots en intérieur: *Indoor jobs*   b. Le métier de chirurgien: *The job of surgeon*

c. Le travail d'équipe: *Teamwork*   d. Jamais seul: *Never alone*   e. Il a pour but de: *It aims to*

f. Soigner: *To treat (a patient)/to care for*

21. Tick the 5 items in the list below which are in the text and cross the 5 which aren't

a. According to √   b. Engineer **X**   c. People √   d. To work √   e. Demanding **X**   f. To start √

g. Team sports **X**   h. They tell me that **X**   i. I hope √   j. Interesting **X**

22. True (T), False (F) or Not mentioned (NM)

a. Sonia is interested in architecture **T**   b. At the moment she studies at university **F**

c. She is not sure which job would be good for her **F**   d. Her friends think she should become a medic **F**

e. She is not at all scared of blood **F**   f. Her parents don't think she should work as a civil servant **F**

g. She prefers indoor jobs **T**   h. She loves scuba diving **NM**

i. She thinks that being an architect is not trendy yet, but will soon become so **F**

23. Find the French equivalent in the text

a. *I dream*: **Je rêve**   b. *Well-paid*: **Bien payé**   c. *I study*: **J'étudie**   d. *I am sure that*: **Je suis sûre que**

e. *It would be*: **Ce serait**   f. *I should try*: **Je devrais essayer**   g. *University*: **Faculté**   h. *Therefore*: **Alors**

i. *To make a career*: **Faire carrière**   j. *Indoor jobs*: **Les boulots en intérieur**

k. *Outdoor/In the open air*: **En plein air**   l. *In the office*: **Au bureau**   m. *The building site*: **Le chantier**

24. Faulty translation – correct the <u>ten</u> errors in the translation of paragraph 4 below

Finally, in order to **become** a good architect, it is necessary to be creative, rigorous and accurate. These are qualities that I **must/have to** develop if I want to **succeed** in this sector. It is **also** important to have some knowledge of history of art and it is imperative to master the **softwares** of technical design. In my **opinion**, it is an activity which is very trendy **currently**, and **so/therefore**, there is a **strong** competition on the architecture job market.

25. Word hunt: find in the text a word for each of the definitions below and translate it into English

a. *A type of job*: **Fonctionnaire**   b. *Another way to say* 'selon moi': **À mon avis**

c. *Opposite of* 'mauvaise': **Bonne**   d. *Another word for* 'boulot': **Travail**

e. *Another way to say* 'copains': **Amis**   f. *Opposite of* 'faible': **Forte**

g. *Another way to say* 'université': **Faculté**

THE LANGUAGE GYM

26. Complete with the missing words

a. Après mes **études**, je voudrais travailler dans la vente   b. Je veux **devenir** avocat ou pilote d'avion

c. Cela me **permettra** de voyager   d. Mes amis me **disent** que je devrais travailler comme instructeur de sport

e. Mes parents pensent que je devrais faire une **carrière** dans la vente   f. Je préfère les emplois en **plein** air

g. Je n'aime pas les **boulots** de bureau   h. Je **rêve** de faire ce métier car cela semble gratifiant et bien **payé**

27. Guided English-to-French translation

a. *Office jobs*: **Des boulots de bureau**   b. *Outdoor jobs*: **Des emplois en plein air**

c. *I would like to become*: **J'aimerais devenir**   d. *My parents tell me*: **Mes parents me disent**

e. *After my studies*: **Après mes études**   f. *It will allow me to*: **Cela me permettra de**

g. *I want to work as*: **Je veux travailler comme**   h. *I dream of this career*: **Je rêve de cette carrière**

i. *In my opinion*: **À mon avis**   j. *I like this profession*: **J'aime cette profession**

k. *It seems demanding*: **Cela semble exigeant**

28. English to French translation (word level)

a. **Études**   b. **Secteur**   c. **Comptable**   d. **Logiciel**   e. **Emploi/boulot/métier**   f. **Gratifiant**   g. **Je veux**

h. **Devenir**   i. **Médecine**   j. **Je préfère**   k. **En plein air**   l. **Bureau**   m. **À mon avis**   n. **Selon moi**

o. **J'aime**   p. **Carrière**   q. **Ma propre entreprise**   r. **Comme instructeur**   s. **Je veux travailler**

t. **J'espère être**

29. Spot and supply the missing word

a. Je voudrais **devenir/être** chirurgienne   b. Je rêve **de** cette carrière   c. Cela me permettra **de** voyager

d. C'est une industrie **en** plein essor   e. Je préfère **les** boulots de bureau

f. À **mon** avis, c'est un boulot gratifiant   g. Je voudrais avoir ma propre **entreprise**

h. Je **veux/voudrais** être avocat ou journaliste   i. J'adore le travail **d'**équipe

30. Translate into French (sentence level translation)

a. Après mes études, je voudrais devenir comptable

b. Selon moi, c'est une industrie en plein essor

c. Je voudrais avoir ma propre entreprise dans le secteur de l'informatique

d. À mon avis, c'est un métier très lucratif

e. Je préfère les boulots en plein air qui sont bien payés et variés

f. Mes parents me disent que je devrais travailler comme instructeur de sport

g. Selon mon frère, je devrais être instructeur de plongée

h. Je ne veux pas travailler comme fonctionnaire parce que je pense que c'est ennuyeux

i. Ce boulot me permettra d'aider les autres et de travailler dans une équipe

j. J'aime cette profession parce que je préfère le travail indépendant

Unit 9. Home, town, neighbourhood and region

1. Match up

Un immeuble – *A block of flats*   Dans la banlieue – *On the outskirts*
Au rez-de-chaussée – *On the ground floor*   Une pièce – *A room*   Des magasins – *Shops*
Une gare routière – *A bus station*   Chez moi – *At home*   Dans ma rue – *In my street*
Mon quartier – *My neighbourhood*   C'est propre – *It's clean*   C'est trop bruyant – *It's too noisy*
Des choses à voir – *Things to see*   C'est très sale – *It's very dirty*   Il y a – *There is/are*

2. Spot and correct the 6 wrong translations

a. Un appartement: *A flat*   b. Une maison: *A house*   c. Dans la banlieue: *On the outskirts*
d. Une cuisine: *A kitchen*   e. Trois chambres: *Three bedrooms*   f. À la campagne: *In the countryside*
g. Une salle à manger: *A dining room*   h. Dans mon quartier: *In my neighbourhood*
i. C'est propre et tranquille: *It's clean and quiet*   j. C'est trop pollué: *It's too polluted*
k. Des espaces verts: *Green spaces*   l. Il y a des plages: *There are beaches*
m. Une zone piétonne: *A pedestrian area*

3. Sentence puzzle

a. J'habite dans une maison à la campagne
b. J'habite dans un appartement dans la banlieue
c. Au premier étage, il y a cinq pièces
d. Chez moi, il y a une cuisine, un salon, une salle à manger et trois chambres
e. Dans ma ville, il y a une gare, des magasins, un centre commercial et un supermarché
f. Dans ma région, il y a beaucoup d'activités pour les touristes

4. Complete the table

English	Français
A train station	Une gare
On the outskirts	**Dans la banlieue**
We have	**Nous avons**
At home	Chez moi
A pedestrian area	Une zone piétonne
It's too noisy	**C'est trop bruyant**
It's very clean	C'est très propre

5. Complete with the correct option

a. Au rez-de-**chaussée**: *On the ground floor*   b. Au premier **étage**: *On the first floor*
c. Il y a six **pièces**: *There are six rooms*   d. C'est **propre** et tranquille: *It's clean and quiet*
e. Dans ma **rue**: *In my street*   f. **Il n'y a pas** d'aéroport: *There isn't an airport*

6. Translate into English

a. J'habite dans: *I live in*   b. Au bord de la mer: *By the sea*   c. Dans la banlieue: *On the outskirts*
d. À la campagne: *In the countryside*   e. Une salle de bain: *A bathroom*   f. Une gare routière: *A bus station*
g. Un supermarché: *A supermarket*   h. Des parcs d'attractions: *Amusement parks*
i. C'est joli et propre: *It's pretty and clean*   j. C'est trop bruyant: *It's too noisy*
k. Mon quartier est sale: *My neighbourhood is dirty*

THE LANGUAGE GYM

7. Definition game (answers in French)

a. Wooden house found in mountain areas: **Chalet**   b. Area on the edge of a town: **La banlieue**

c. A building containing books: **Bibliothèque**   d. District within a town: **Quartier**

e. Land in rural areas: **Campagne**   f. Not clean: **Sale**   g. An enclosed shopping area: **Centre commercial**

h. A small establishment serving drinks and snacks: **Café**   i. Free from noise: **Tranquille**

j. Affected by pollution: **Pollué**   k. Strip of land covered in sand: **Plage**

8. Wordsearch: find the French translation of the words below

	P		M	A	G	A	S	I	N	S						P	
	L				C	A	M	P	A	G	N	E		P		I	B
	A		S	U	P	E	R	M	A	R	C	H	É	R		S	R
	G						E							O		C	U
R	E	Z	D	E	C	H	A	U	S	S	É	E		P		I	Y
					B	A	N	L	I	E	U	E		R		N	A
		B	I	B	L	I	O	T	H	È	Q	U	E	E		E	N
A	U	B	O	R	D	D	E	L	A	M	E	R					T

supermarket: **supermarché**   library: **bibliothèque**   beach: **plage**

block of flats: **immeuble**   by the sea: **au bord de la mer**   noisy: **bruyant**

outskirts: **banlieue**   swimming pool: **piscine**   clean: **propre**

ground floor: **rez-de-chaussée**   countryside: **campagne**   shops: **magasins**

9. Complete with the missing vowels

a. **Immeuble**: *Block of flats*   b. **Banlieue**: *Outskirts*   c. **Quartier**: *Neighbourhood*

d. **Gare routière**: *Bus station*   e. **Chez moi**: *At home*   f. **Au premier étage**: *On the first floor*

g. **Des choses à voir**: *Things to see*   h. **Salle de bain**: *Bathroom*

10. Split phrases

Mon quartier est	**très propre et tranquille**
Dans ma rue,	**il y a un café**
Malheureusement, nous	**n'avons pas d'aéroport**
Il y a beaucoup	**de choses à faire**
J'habite dans un	**grand immeuble en ville**
Au rez-de-chaussée, il y a	**une cuisine et un salon**
J'aime ma ville	**car c'est joli et pas pollué**
Je déteste mon village car	**c'est sale et bruyant**

11. Gapped English-to-French translation

a. Dans ma **rue**: *In my street*   b. C'est **joli** et très **propre**: *It's pretty and very clean*

c. J'habite dans un **appartement**: *I live in a flat*   d. **Chez** moi, il y a huit **pièces**: *At home, there are 8 rooms*

e. Mon **quartier** est **bruyant**: *My neighbourhood is noisy*   f. J'**adore** ma **ville**: *I love my town*

g. **Il y a** une gare **routière**: *There is a bus station*   h. Une **maison** à la **campagne**: *A house in the countryside*

i. **Pas** trop **pollué**: *Not too polluted*   j. Des choses à **voir**: *Things to see*

THE LANGUAGE GYM

12. Spot and supply the missing words

a. C'est sale **et** bruyant   b. J'habite dans **un** immeuble moderne   c. Mon quartier **est** propre et tranquille

d. Nous n'avons **pas** de piscine   e. Au premier **étage**, il y a trois chambres   f. Il n'y a pas **de** zone piétonne

g. Dans ma région, il y a beaucoup d'espaces **verts**   h. J'habite dans une maison **à** la campagne

i. Chez **moi**, il y a une cuisine et un salon   j. Il y beaucoup de choses **à** faire

k. J'adore mon village car **c'est** joli et propre

13. Complete with the missing letters

a. C'est tro**p** bruyant   b. Au bor**d** de la mer   c. Au rez-de-chaussé**e**   d. Dans ma ru**e**, il y a un petit café

e. J'**h**abite dans un im**m**euble en ville   f. C'est très joli, mais trop pollu**é**   g. C'es**t** dans la **b**anlieue de ma ville

h. Ma maison est à la **c**ampag**n**e

14. Phrase anagrams

a. J'habite dans un joli chalet   b. Chez moi, il y a sept pièces

c. Au premier étage, il y a une cuisine et une salle à manger   d. Dans mon quartier, il y a une bibliothèque

e. J'aime ma ville car c'est propre   f. Je déteste ma ville car c'est trop pollué

g. Ma maison est dans la banlieue   h. Mon appartement est au bord de la mer

15. Complete with an appropriate word

a. J'habite **dans** un chalet à la **montagne**   b. Au premier **étage**, il y a trois chambres

c. Dans ma ville, nous **avons** beaucoup de cafés   d. Il y a beaucoup de **choses** à faire pour les jeunes

e. Malheureusement, mon quartier est trop **bruyant/sale/pollué**   f. Il n'y a pas de zone **piétonne**

g. Chez **moi**, il y a dix **pièces**   h. Dans ma ville, il y a une gare **routière**

i. Il y a un centre **commercial** près de **chez** moi   j. J'aime mon quartier, car c'est **joli** et **tranquille/propre**

k. Ma maison est dans la **banlieue** de ma ville

l. Au **premier/deuxième** étage, il y a deux **chambres/salles de bain**

16. Guided translation

a. *Unfortunately*: **Malheureusement**   b. *My town is clean*: **Ma ville est propre**

c. *It's very noisy*: **C'est très bruyant**   d. *A block of flats*: Un **immeuble**   e. *A supermarket*: Un **supermarché**

f. *We have a kitchen*: **Nous avons une cuisine**   g. *Amusement parks*: Des **parcs d'attractions**

h. *On the first floor*: Au **premier étage**   i. *Green spaces*: Des **espaces verts**

j. *A pedestrian area*: Une **zone piétonne**   k. *Two bathrooms*: **Deux salles de bain**

l. *A lot of shops*: **Beaucoup de magasins**

17. Find the French equivalent in the text (paragraph 1)

a. *Today*: **Aujourd'hui**   b. *I am going to talk about*: **Je vais parler de**   c. *Where*: **Où**

d. *A flat*: **Un appartement**   e. *In town*: **En ville**   f. *At home*: **Chez moi**   g. *Floors*: **Étages**

h. *We have*: **Nous avons**   i. *Eight rooms*: **Huit pièces**   j. *On the ground floor*: **Au rez-de-chaussée**

k. *A dining room*: **Une salle à manger**

18. Complete the translation of paragraph 2

On the second **floor**, there is my parents' **bedroom**, my **sister**'s bedroom and **my** bedroom. There is **also** a big **bathroom**. I **like** my **flat** because it's **bright** and modern. It's also well **located**, near some **shops** and the botanic **garden** and it's **five** minutes away on **foot** from my **school**. My favourite **room** is my bedroom because it's **clean**, tidy and **spacious**.

19. Spot and supply the missing words in this wrong version of paragraph 3 (12 words)

Ma ville **s'appelle** Annecy et **c'est** situé **en** Haute-Savoie, un département **des** Alpes françaises. J'adore **ma** ville car c'est très joli **et** toujours propre. En hiver, **on** peut faire du ski et **en** été, on peut nager dans **le** lac, faire du vélo ou **du** parapente. Malheureusement, il n'y a pas d'aéroport **à** Annecy, **alors** il faut aller prendre l'avion à Lyon.

20. Translate into English the phrases below taken from paragraph 3

a. C'est situé: ***It's located***   b. C'est très joli: ***It's very pretty***   c. Toujours propre: ***Always clean***

d. En hiver: ***In the winter***   e. En été: ***In the summer***   f. On peut nager: ***You can swim***

g. Prendre l'avion: ***To take a plane***

21. Tick the 5 items in the list below which are in the text and cross the 5 which aren't

a. To talk √   b. Waterskiing **X**   c. Well located √   d. To swim √   e. In autumn **X**   f. Hiking √
g. Polluted **X**   h. Noisy **X**   i. Tomorrow **X**   j. Sunset √

22. True (T), False (F) or Not mentioned (NM)

a. Maxime lives in a house by the sea **T**   b. His town is located in the south of France **F**

c. He likes water sports **T**   d. Maxime has two siblings **T**   e. He has a dog at home **NM**

f. There is an attic in his house **T**   g. His neighbourhood is clean **T**   h. There is a train station near his house **F**

i. There isn't much to do for youngsters in La Rochelle **F**   j. He can go swimming in the sea in the summer **T**

k. There isn't a mall in his town **F**

23. Find the French equivalent in the text

a. *By the sea*: **Au bord de la mer**   b. *It's located*: **C'est situé**   c. *West*: **Ouest**   d. *I can do*: **Je peux faire**

e. *When I want*: **Quand je veux**   f. *On the ground floor*: **Au rez-de-chaussée**

g. *A games room*: **Une salle de jeux**   h. *An attic*: **Un grenier**   i. *To store things*: **Pour ranger des affaires**

j. *Practical*: **Pratique**   k. *It's too noisy*: **C'est trop bruyant**   l. *Pedestrian streets*: **Rues piétonnes**

24. Faulty translation – correct the <u>ten</u> errors in the translation of paragraph 4 below

I love La Rochelle because there are a lot of things to **do** for young people. You can go to the **beach** and swim in the **sea** in the summer and in the winter, you can go to the cinema or to the **mall**. In my region, there are a **lot of** activities for tourists. They can for example **visit** the aquarium or **walk** in the **old** town to **see** historical monuments and take some photos of the pretty **pedestrian** streets.

25. Word hunt: find in the text a word for each of the definitions below and translate it into English

a. *A type of habitation*: **Maison**   b. *A cardinal direction*: **Ouest**   c. *An embarcation designed by the Inuit*: **Kayak**

d. *A room inside the roof of a building*: **Grenier**   e. *A room used for playing*: **Salle de jeux**

f. *A synonym of* 'quelquefois': **Parfois**   g. *The verb coming from* 'promenade': **Se promener**

26. Complete with the missing words

a. Je vais **parler** de là où j'habite   b. Chez moi, il y a deux **étages**   c. C'est bien **situé**   d. Nous avons dix **pièces**

e. Ma ville est **propre** et **tranquille**   f. On peut faire de la **randonnée**   g. En **hiver**, on peut faire du ski

h. En été, on peut **nager** à la **plage**   i. Dans mon quartier, il y a une **épicerie**

j. C'est trop **bruyant** pendant le week-end   k. On peut se **promener** dans la vieille ville

27. Guided English-to-French translation

a. *It's well located*: **C'est bien situé**   b. *To take some photos*: **Prendre des photos**

c. *Sometimes, it's too noisy*: **Parfois, c'est trop bruyant**   d. *You can swim*: **On peut nager**

e. *In my neighbourhood*: **Dans mon quartier**   f. *My brother's bedroom*: **La chambre de mon frère**

g. *By the sea*: **Au bord de la mer**   h. *To walk in town*: **Se promener en ville**

i. *A lot of people*: **Beaucoup de monde**   j. *There isn't an airport*: **Il n'y a pas d'aéroport**

k. *We have a garden*: **Nous avons un jardin**

28. Translate into French (sentence level translation)

a. J'aime mon quartier, mais parfois c'est trop bruyant pendant le week-end

b. Chez moi, nous avons huit pièces et il y a deux étages

c. J'adore ma région parce qu'il y a beaucoup de choses à faire pour les jeunes

d. En été, on peut aller à la plage et nager dans la mer. C'est génial!

e. Dans ma rue, il y a beaucoup de magasins et de cafés. Il y a aussi toujours beaucoup de monde

f. J'aime habiter à la montagne parce que je peux faire de la randonnée

g. J'adore habiter près de la mer parce que je peux faire des sports nautiques quand je veux

h. Au rez-de-chaussée, nous avons une cuisine, un salon et une salle à manger

i. Je n'aime pas ma ville parce que c'est sale, bruyant, dangereux et pollué

j. Dans ma région, il y a beaucoup d'activités pour les touristes

29. Translate the following paragraphs into French

Je m'appelle Audrey et j'habite à Saint-Tropez dans le sud de la France. J'habite dans une grande maison au bord de la mer avec ma famille. Chez moi, au rez-de-chaussée il y a une cuisine, un salon, une salle à manger, la chambre de mes parents et une salle de bain.

Au premier étage,il y a cinq pièces: la chambre de ma sœur, ma chambre, une salle de bain, une salle de jeux et un bureau. Ma pièce préférée, c'est ma chambre parce que c'est lumineux, bien rangé et spacieux.

J'aime ma ville parce que c'est joli et propre et il y a beaucoup de choses à faire pour les jeunes. Malheureusement, en été il y a beaucoup de monde et parfois c'est trop bruyant parce qu'il y a beaucoup de circulation.

Unit 10. Travel and tourism

1. Match up

L'année dernière – ***Last year***   Cet été – ***This summer***   Je suis allé(e) – ***I went***   J'irai – ***I will go***
Pendant les vacances – ***During the holidays***   J'ai logé dans – ***I stayed in***   J'ai voyagé – ***I travelled***
En avion – ***By plane***   En Écosse – ***To Scotland***   J'ai passé – ***I spent***   C'était – ***It was***
Deux semaines – ***Two weeks***   J'ai loué un vélo – ***I rented a bike***   Ce sera génial – ***It will be great***

2. Spot and correct the 6 wrong translations

a. Je suis allé en Suisse: *I went to Switzerland*   b. J'ai voyagé: *I travelled*   c. En avion: *By **plane***
d. J'ai loué une voiture: *I rented a **car***   e. J'ai passé deux semaines: *I spent two weeks*
f. Le matin: *In the **morning***   g. Pendant les vacances: *During the holidays*   h. Ce sera génial: *It will be great*
i. J'ai voyagé en bateau: *I travelled by **boat***   j. Une auberge de jeunesse: *A youth hostel*
k. J'ai bronzé: *I sunbathed*   l. L'année prochaine: *Next year*   m. Je passerai un mois: *I will spend one **month***

3. Sentence puzzle

a. Je suis allée en vacances en Allemagne avec ma famille
b. Je voudrais aller en vacances en Suisse car c'est très joli
c. L'année prochaine, j'irai en Écosse pour voir mes grands-parents
d. J'ai logé dans une auberge de jeunesse
e. J'ai passé deux semaines en Espagne. C'était génial!
f. J'ai voyagé en voiture et puis j'ai loué un vélo

4. Complete the table

Perfect tense	Future
Je suis allé(e)	**J'irai**
J'ai loué	Je louerai
J'ai passé	Je passerai
C'était **(imperfect)**	**Ce sera**
J'ai fait	Je ferai
Je suis sorti(e)	Je sortirai
J'ai logé	**Je logerai**

5. Complete with the correct option

a. Une auberge de **jeunesse**: *A youth hostel*   b. L'année **dernière**: *Last year*   c. Je suis **sorti**: *I went out*
d. C'**était** génial: *It was great*   e. J'ai **bronzé** à la plage: *I sunbathed at the beach*
f. Je **voyagerai** en bateau: *I will travel by boat*

6. Translate into English

a. I will travel by train   b. It was very interesting   c. In the afternoon   d. I rented a car   e. Next year
f. I will spend one week   g. I will travel by plane   h. I will go to Scotland   i. It will be great
j. During the holidays   k. I went to England

7. Definition game

a. Vehicle designed to travel on water: **Bateau**   b. Vehicle designed for air travel: **Avion**
c. A period of seven days: **Semaine**   d. A time when someone is free to travel: **Vacances**
e. The contrary of "intéressant": **Ennuyeux**   f. A large area of water surrounded by land: **Lac**
g. A building containing historical objects: **Musée**   h. A period of about four weeks: **Mois**
i. The northernmost country in the UK: **Écosse**   j. The period that starts after lunch: **Après-midi**
k. The activity of visiting places: J'ai fait du **tourisme**

THE LANGUAGE GYM

8. Wordsearch: find the French translation of the words below

E	R			V	O	Y	A	G	E	R	A	I				V	
N	E						I	N	T	É	R	E	S	S	A	N	T
N	L		E	S	P	A	G	N	E						C		
U	A		V	R	A	I	M	E	N	T		P	E	N	D	A	N	T
Y	X										S	E	M	A	I	N	E
E	A	P	R	È	S	M	I	D	I						C		
U	N				A	N	G	L	E	T	E	R	R	E			
X	T		V	O	I	T	U	R	E					S			

holidays: **vacances** during: **pendant** car: **voiture**
interesting: **intéressant** week: **semaine** really: **vraiment**
England: **Angleterre** afternoon: **après-midi** relaxing: **relaxant**
I will travel: je **voyagerai** Spain: **Espagne** boring: **ennuyeux**

9. Complete with the missing vowels
a. **Relaxant**: *Relaxing*   b. **Après-midi**: *Afternoon*   c. **Je sortirai**: *I will go out*   d. **Je logerai**: *I will stay*
e. **Je voyagerai**: *I will travel*   f. **Une semaine**: *One week*   g. **J'ai voyagé**: *I travelled*   h. **En bateau**: *By boat*

10. Split phrases
J'ai voyagé en **avion. C'était relaxant!**   Je suis allée **en Espagne. C'était génial!**
Je voyagerai pendant **quatre heures**   Je voudrais **aller en vacances en Suisse**
J'ai bronzé à la **plage tous les jours**   Ensuite, j'ai loué **un vélo**

11. Gapped English-to-French translation
a. J'ai **voyagé** en avion: *I travelled by plane*   b. Cet **été**, j'irai en France: *This summer, I'll go to France*
c. J'ai **logé** dans un hôtel: *I stayed in a hotel*   d. J'ai **loué** une **voiture**: *I rented a car*
e. J'ai visité des **musées**: *I visited some museums*   f. J'ai **passé** un **mois** là-bas: *I spent one month there*
g. C'**était** vraiment **relaxant**: *It was really relaxing*   h. Ce **sera** génial: *It will be great*
i. J'**irai** en **Suisse**: *I will go to Switzerland*   j. Je **voyagerai** en **bateau**: *I will travel by boat*
k. L'année **prochaine**: *Next year*

12. Spot and supply the missing words
a. J'ai bronzé **à** la plage   b. Je suis allé **en** Espagne   c. J'ai loué **une** voiture de sport
d. J'ai passé un mois **au** bord de la mer   e. J'ai voyagé **en** train, c'était confortable
f. Le soir, je **suis** sorti au restaurant   g. J'ai logé **dans** une auberge de jeunesse
h. Je voudrais aller **en** vacances en Suisse   i. J'ai visité beaucoup **de** monuments
j. Je louerai **un** vélo et j'irai **à** la plage   k. Pendant **les** vacances, je logerai dans un hôtel

13. Complete with the missing letters
a. L'après-midi, j'ai bronz**é**   b. J'ai fai**t** d**u** tourisme   c. Je f**e**rai des visites guidée**s**
d. J'ai log**é** dans un camping   e. C'étai**t** asse**z** ennuyeux   f. Le s**o**ir, je suis sor**ti** en boîte
g. Je lou**e**rai une voi**tu**re   h. J'ai **p**assé un mois à la monta**g**ne

14. Phrase anagrams
a. Cet été, j'irai en Écosse   b. J'ai fait du tourisme   c. J'ai logé dans une auberge de jeunesse
d. J'ai voyagé en avion   e. Le soir, je suis sorti au restaurant   f. Je bronzerai à la plage
g. J'irai en Espagne   h. Je voyagerai en train et ensuite je louerai un vélo

THE LANGUAGE GYM

15. Complete with an appropriate word

a. J'ai visité des **monuments** historiques   b. Le matin, j'ai **fait** du tourisme

c. J'ai **passé** deux semaines en Espagne   d. C'**était** génial, car il y avait beaucoup d'attractions

e. L'après-midi, j'ai **bronzé** à la plage   f. L'année **prochaine**, j'irai en Angleterre

g. Je voyagerai en train et ensuite je **louerai** un vélo   h. Le matin, j'ai fait des visites **guidées**

i. Je logerai dans une **auberge** de jeunesse   j. Cette année, je **voudrais** aller en vacances

k. Je passerai un **mois** à la montagne   l. Ce **sera** vraiment relaxant

16. Guided translation

a. *Five days*: **Cinq jours**   b. *By the sea*: **Au bord de la mer**   c. *Two weeks*: **Deux semaines**

d. *In the afternoon*: **L'après-midi**   e. *A youth hostel*: **Une auberge de jeunesse**

f. *I will go to Spain*: **J'irai en Espagne**   g. *I will travel*: **Je voyagerai**

h. *I will spend one month*: **Je passerai un mois**   i. *I did some sightseeing*: **J'ai fait du tourisme**

j. *At the beach*: **À la plage**   k. *I rented a bike*: **J'ai loué un vélo**   l. *I would like to go*: **Je voudrais aller**

17. Find the French equivalent in paragraph 1

a. *Germany*: **Allemagne**   b. *We spent*: **Nous avons passé**   c. *Two weeks*: **Deux semaines.**   d. *There*: **Là-bas**

e. *We stayed*: **Nous avons logé**   f. *Three-star*: **Trois étoiles**   g. *First*: **Première**   h. *Afterwards*: **Ensuite**

i. *A youth hostel*: **Une auberge de jeunesse**   j. *Second*: **Deuxième**

18. Complete the translation of paragraph 2

It was the first **time** that I **went** to Germany **and** I was pleasantly **surprised** because **there were** a lot of activities to do for **young people** and loads of things to see too. I **travelled** by **car** and the journey took seven **hours**. It was quite **tiring**, but **very** comfortable.

19. Spot and supply the <u>eight</u> missing words in this wrong version of paragraph 3

Pendant **la** première semaine, nous étions en ville **à** Cologne. C'est une ville superbe **avec** beaucoup de monuments magnifiques. Nous **avons** visité la cathédrale et quelques musées **et** nous avons fait le tour de **la** vieille ville à pied. Nous avons aussi fait une visite guidée à vélo et j'ai adoré **ça** car c'était original et nous avons vu des endroits fabuleux tout **en** faisant du sport en plein air.

20. Translate into English the words and phrases below taken from paragraph 3

a. Pendant: **During**   b. Nous avons visité: **We visited**   c. Une visite guidée: **A guided visit**

d. Quelques musées: **A few museums**   e. La vieille ville: **The old town**   f. À pied: **On foot**

g. Endroits: **Places**

21. Tick the 5 items in the list below which are in the text and cross the 5 which aren't

a. Next year **X**   b. I went **√**   c. We stayed **√**   d. Three-star hotel **X**   e. Car **√**   f. Tired **X**

g. Boring **X**   h. Outdoor **√**   i. Relaxing **√**   j. Rain **X**

22. True (T), False (F) or Not mentioned (NM)

a. Sophie went on holidays to Spain **T**   b. She found Spanish people noisy **F**   c. She travelled by car **F**

d. She spent three days in Barcelona **T**   e. She visited a cathedral **T**   f. She didn't like Spanish architecture **F**

g. After Barcelona, she travelled to the north of Spain **F**   h. She found that Sevilla was an ugly city **F**

i. She went on holidays with her boyfriend **T**   j. She met with some old friends in Sevilla **NM**

k. Next year, she would like to go to Scotland **F**

THE LANGUAGE GYM

23. Find the French equivalent in the text

a. *For the first time*: **Pour la première fois**   b. *There were*: **Il y avait**   c. *Until late*: **Jusqu'à tard**
d. *The night*: **La nuit**   e. *My flight*: **Mon vol**   f. *To go for a swim*: **Se baigner**   g. *I took*: **J'ai pris**
h. *I found*: **J'ai trouvé**   i. *Well-known*: **Connus**   j. *The same country*: **Le même pays**
k. *Until 3 o'clock in the morning*: **Jusqu'à trois heures du matin**   l. *Unforgettable*: **Inoubliables**

24. Faulty translation – correct the <u>eight</u> errors in the translation of paragraph 4 below

I ate at the restaurant every **evening** and my **boyfriend** and I went out to some **night** bars and then clubbing until **three** o'clock in the morning. They were **unforgettable** holidays and next **year** I would like to **return** to Spain and this time I will **go to** Madrid.

25. Word hunt – find in the text a word for each of the definitions below and translate it into English

a. *A word related to "premium"*: **première**   b. *The word for "welcoming"*: **accueillants**
c. *A journey in a plane*: **vol**   d. *An adjective for "extremely large"*: **gigantesque**
e. *The expression for "one more time"*: **encore une fois**   f. *An adjective meaning "well-known"*: **connus**
g. *An area of land that has its own language*: **pays**

26. Complete with the missing words

a. Ce **que** j'ai adoré   b. Mon **endroit** préféré   c. Aller se **baigner**   d. **Jusqu'à** tard
e. Mon vol a **duré** deux heures   f. J'ai **pris** le train   g. J'ai **voyagé** en avion
h. C'étaient des vacances **inoubliables**   i. Il y **avait** beaucoup d'animations
j. J'ai **mangé** au restaurant   k. Les gens étaient **accueillants**

27. Guided English-to-French translation

a. *We spent*: **Nous avons passé**   b. *We stayed*: **Nous avons logé**   c. *There were*: **Il y avait**
d. *It was quite tiring*: **C'était assez fatigant**   e. *We visited*: **Nous avons visité**   f. *A cruise*: **Une croisière**
g. *I swam*: **J'ai nagé**   h. *I sunbathed*: **J'ai bronzé**   i. *My favourite place*: **Mon endroit préféré**
j. *Very near*: **Très près**   k. *To go for a swim*: **Aller se baigner**

28. Translate into French (sentence level translation)

a. L'année dernière, je suis allé(e) en vacances en Écosse. C'était génial!
b. J'ai voyagé en avion et ensuite j'ai loué une voiture
c. Le trajet a duré trois heures et c'était assez fatigant, mais confortable
d. J'ai logé dans un hôtel et c'était très près du centre-ville
e. J'ai fait une visite guidée de tous les monuments les plus connus. C'était intéressant
f. Le soir, j'ai mangé au restaurant et je suis sorti(e) jusqu'à tard
g. J'ai aussi visité beaucoup de musées, mais à mon avis, c'était un peu ennuyeux
h. L'année prochaine, j'irai à Glasgow et je voyagerai à l'ouest du pays
i. Je passerai deux semaines au bord de la mer
j. C'étaient des vacances inoubliables. Je voudrais retourner en Écosse l'été prochain

29. Translate the following paragraphs into French

L'année dernière, je suis allé(e) en vacances en Suisse pour la première fois. J'ai voyagé en avion et le vol était assez fatigant, mais très confortable. Le trajet a duré quatre heures.

J'ai logé dans une auberge de jeunesse à Genève et j'ai trouvé que les gens étaient accueillants. Le premier jour, j'ai fait une visite guidée en bus. Mon endroit préféré était la vieille ville car c'était très joli et propre.

Le deuxième jour, j'ai loué un vélo et je suis allé(e) au lac. J'ai bronzé et j'ai nagé, c'était génial! Le soir, j'ai mangé au restaurant et puis je suis sorti(e) avec des amis.

L'année prochaine, je voudrais retourner en Suisse, mais en hiver. Je voudrais essayer le ski car cela a l'air amusant et un peu risqué aussi.

THE LANGUAGE GYM

Unit 11. Sport

1. Match up
Parfois – **Sometimes**   Les sports d'équipe – **Team sports**   Je fais – **I do**   La voile – **Sailing**

Après le collège – **After school**   Quand je peux – **When I can**   Motivant – **Motivating**

La musculation – **Bodybuilding**   Je ferai – **I will do**   Exaltant – **Thrilling**   J'ai gagné – **I won**

L'escalade – **Rock climbing**   La plongée – **Scuba diving**   J'ai perdu – **I lost**

2. Spot and correct the 6 wrong translations
a. Quand je peux: *When I can*   b. Je ferai: *I will do*   c. C'est plus motivant: *It's **more** motivating*

d. Je joue au basket: *I play basketball*   e. D'habitude: *Usually*   f. Je m'entraîne: *I train*

g. Le week-end dernier: ***Last** weekend*   h. J'ai gagné: ***I won***   i. Le patin à glace: *Ice skating*

j. Deux fois par semaine: *Twice a week*   k. Je ne joue jamais: *I **never** play*

l. Hier: *Yesterday*   m. L'équitation: ***Horse riding***

3. Sentence puzzle
a. Une fois par semaine, je joue au foot   b. Je préfère les sports d'équipe car c'est plus amusant

c. Parfois, je fais de la natation   d. Je ne joue jamais au golf   e. Hier, j'ai fait de la voile

f. Demain, je ferai de la musculation

4. Complete the table

English	Français
At the swimming pool	À la piscine
I don't play	**Je ne joue pas**
I train	Je m'entraîne
Rock climbing	**Escalade**
Scuba diving	La plongée
I lost	J'ai perdu
Team sports	**Les sports d'équipe**

5. Complete with the correct option
a. Tous les **samedis**: *Every Saturday*   b. Je fais du **vélo**: *I do cycling*   c. Je voudrais **essayer**: *I would like to try*

d. C'est trop **fatigant**: *It's too tiring*   e. J'ai fait de la **randonnée**: *I did hiking*   f. Quand je **peux**: *When I can*

6. Translate into English
a. ***I never play***   b. ***It's too tiring***   c. ***Sometimes***   d. ***I did sailing***   e. ***It's more motivating***   f. ***Twice a week***

g. ***My favourite sport***   h. ***I train one hour per day***   i. ***It's too difficult***   j. ***When I have the time***

k. ***I will do bodybuilding***

7. Definition game (answers in French)
a. Underwater sport: **Plongée**   b. Table tennis in French: **Ping-pong**

c. The sport of climbing on rocks: **Escalade**   d. The sport of swimming: **Natation**

e. The day after today: **Demain**   f. A French adverb coming from "habit": **D'habitude**

g. A sport played with a cork: **Badminton**   h. A number of people playing as a group: **Équipe**

i. Exercises you do to build muscles: **Musculation**   j. Long walk in the countryside: **Randonnée**

k. To attempt to do something: **Essayer**

THE LANGUAGE GYM

8. Wordsearch: find the French translation of the words below

	T		E	S	C	A	L	A	D	E								
E	N	T	R	A	Î	N	E					P	R	É	F	È	R	E
	A			F	A	T	I	G	A	N	T		Q	U	A	N	D	
	V		P	L	O	N	G	É	E				U					
D	I	V	E	R	T	I	S	S	A	N	T		I					
	T							P	I	N	G	P	O	N	G			
C	O	M	P	É	T	I	T	I	F			E						
	M	U	S	C	U	L	A	T	I	O	N							

bodybuilding: **musculation**　　table tennis: **ping-pong**　　when: **quand**

I prefer: je **préfère**　　tiring: **fatigant**　　entertaining: **divertissant**

rock climbing: **escalade**　　team: **équipe**　　I train: je m'**entraîne**

motivating: **motivant**　　scuba diving: **plongée**　　competitive: **compétitif**

9. Complete with the missing vowels

a. **Amusant**: *Fun*　b. **De la voile**: *Sailing*　c. **D'habitude**: *Usually*　d. **De l'athlétisme**: *Athletics*

e. **Je jouerai**: *I will play*　f. **De la plongée**: *Scuba diving*　g. **J'ai gagné**: *I won*　h. **Si je pouvais**: *If I could*

10. Split phrases

Tous les samedis, **je joue au basket**　Après le collège, je **fais de la natation**　Hier, j'ai fait **de la randonnée**

Le week-end prochain, **je jouerai au badminton**　Le week-end dernier, **j'ai joué au rugby**

Je ne joue **jamais au golf**　Je m'entraîne **deux fois par semaine**　Si je pouvais, je voudrais **essayer le ski**

11. Gapped English-to-French translation

a. J'ai **fait** de la voile: *I did sailing*　b. Parfois, je **joue** au foot: *Sometimes, I play football*

c. Je m'**entraîne** souvent: *I often train*　d. J'ai fait de la **randonnée**: *I did hiking*

e. Demain, je **ferai** du vélo: *Tomorrow, I will do cycling*　f. Je **ne** joue **pas** au tennis: *I don't play tennis*

g. Je **ne** joue **jamais** au golf: *I never play golf*　h. J'adore l'**escalade**: *I love rock climbing*

i. Quand je **peux**: *When I can*　j. **Quand** j'ai le **temps**: *When I have the time*

k. Mon sport **préféré**: *My favourite sport*

12. Spot and supply the missing words

a. Le week-end dernier, j'ai joué **au** golf　b. Hier, j'ai fait de **la** plongée　c. Demain, je ferai **de** la musculation

d. Je **ne** joue jamais au tennis　e. Mon sport préféré, **c'est** l'escalade　f. Je préfère **les** sports individuels

g. Je n'aime pas les sports **d'**équipe　h. La plupart **du** temps, je m'entraîne au stade

i. Si **je** pouvais, je voudrais essayer le ski　j. Quand je peux, je fais **du** vélo　k. Cela **a** l'air divertissant

13. Complete with the missing letters

a. Car c'est trop fatigant　b. J'adore la musculation　c. Je voudrais essayer la plongée

d. J'aime les sports d'équipe　e. Car cela a l'air amusant　f. Hier j'ai joué au foot

g. Demain, je jouerai au badminton　h. Le tennis, c'est trop difficile

14. Phrase anagrams

a. Le soir, je fais de la boxe avec mon ami　b. Quand je peux, je fais de la natation

c. Mon sport préféré, c'est l'escalade　d. En général, je m'entraîne au stade

e. Hier, j'ai joué au ping-pong　f. Demain, je ferai de la musculation

g. Hier, j'ai joué au foot, mais j'ai perdu　h. La plupart du temps, je m'entraîne au gymnase

50

 **THE LANGUAGE GYM**

15. Complete with an appropriate word

a. Quand je **peux**, je fais de la boxe   b. Hier, j'ai **joué** au tennis, c'était amusant!

c. Demain, je **ferai** de la musculation   d. La **plupart** du temps, je m'entraîne au stade

e. Je ne joue **pas/jamais** au golf, car c'est trop difficile   f. D'habitude, je m'**entraîne** une heure par jour

g. Demain, je **jouerai** au badminton, ce sera génial!   h. Je joue au rugby deux **fois** par semaine

i. Je n'aime pas la natation, c'est **trop/très** fatigant   j. Demain, je ferai de la voile **avec** ma sœur

k. Parfois, je **fais** de l'athlétisme   l. Je préfère les sports d'**équipe** car c'est plus motivant

16. Guided translation

a. *Every Saturday*: **Tous les samedis**   b. *At the gym*: **Au gymnase**   c. *Once a week:* **Une fois par semaine**

d. *It's too tiring*: **C'est trop fatigant**   e. *Most of the time*: **La plupart du temps**

f. *I would like to try*: **Je voudrais essayer**   g. *I will do*: **Je ferai**   h. *It look fun*: **Cela a l'air amusant**

i. *It's quite risky*: **C'est assez risqué**   j. *It's thrilling*: **C'est exaltant**   k. *At the swimming pool*: **À la piscine**

l. *With my friend*: **Avec mon ami(e)**

17. Find the French equivalent in the text (paragraph 1)

a. *Sporty*: **Sportive**   b. *I train*: **Je m'entraîne**   c. *My favourite sport*: **Mon sport préféré**   d. *I play*: **Je joue**

e. *My local club*: **Mon club local**   f. *Since*: **Depuis**   g. *I am also part of*: **Je fais aussi partie de**

h. *Team*: **Équipe**   i. *Last year*: **L'année dernière**

18. Complete the translation of paragraph 2

Every **Monday**, I do **athletics** at the stadium with my **teammates**. On **Tuesdays**, I do **bodybuilding** at the **gym**. On Wednesdays, I **rest** at home and I do my **homework**, I **read** or I **study** my favourite **subjects**. On Thursdays, I **train** with my **team** at the **sports centre** near my house. Finally, on Fridays, I do **swimming** at the local **swimming pool** with my **brother** and my **sister**.

19. Spot and supply the ten missing words in this wrong version of paragraph 3

Tous **les** samedis, j'ai un match. Parfois **nous** jouons à domicile et j'adore **ça** car nous avons tous nos supporters dans la salle **de** sport et c'est motivant. Sinon, nous jouons **à** l'extérieur, quelquefois **très** loin alors c'est fatigant car **il** faut voyager pendant des heures **en** car. Hier nous avons gagné et c'était génial car nous avons battu une des **meilleures** équipes de **notre** région.

20. Translate into English the words and phrases below taken from paragraph 3

a. J'ai un match: *I have a match/game*   b. Parfois: *Sometimes*   c. À domicile: *At home (for sports games)*

d. À l'extérieur: *Outside*   e. Quelquefois: *Sometimes*   f. Loin: *Far*   g. Nous avons battu: *We beat*

21. Tick the 5 items in the list below which are in the text and cross the 5 which aren't

a. I train √   b. Most of the time **X**   c. Bodybuilding √   d. Individual sports **X**   e. Tiring **X**

f. Motivating √   g. Interesting **X**   h. Risky √   i. Tomorrow **X**   j. I would like to try √

22. True (T), False (F) or Not mentioned (NM)

a. Olivier lives in Brittany **T**   b. His town is located near the Mediterranean Sea **F**   c. He loves sailing **T**

d. He owns a boat with his brother **NM**   e. He trains twice a week **T**   f. Last weekend, he lost a race **F**

g. Next weekend, he will go to Vendée **T**   h. He would like to try martial arts **T**   i. He loves racket sports **F**

j. He has a girlfriend called Julie **NM**   k. He thinks rock climbing is boring **F**

THE LANGUAGE GYM

23. Find the French equivalent in the text

a. *I am passionate about*: **Je suis passionné de**   b. *A place*: **Un endroit**   c. *Wind*: **Vent**

d. *In the summer*: **En été**   e. *Recreational*: **Récréatif**   f. *I am part of*: **Je fais partie du**   g. *I will go*: **J'irai**

h. *Race*: **Course**   i. *To find*: **Trouver**   j. *If I could*: **Si je pouvais**   k. *Quite risky*: **Assez risqué**

l. *At the same time*: **En même temps**

24. Faulty translation – correct the <u>ten</u> errors in the translation of paragraph 4 below

If I could, I would like to **try** martial arts because I am fascinated by **combat** sports and Bruce Lee's films. **I never** play **racket** sports because I am **bad,** and I find this **boring**. I would also like to do **rock climbing** in the **mountains** one day as it's rather **risky** and **technical** at the same time.

25. Word hunt – find in the text a word for each of the definitions below and translate it into English

a. The verb "to navigate" in French: **Naviguer**   b. The word for "marina": **Port de plaisance**

c. A word for "crewmate": **Équipier**   d. The French word for "start": **Départ**

e. "Around the world" in French: **Autour du monde**   f. An adjective meaning "bad": **Mauvais**

g. The expression for "while waiting": **En attendant**

26. Complete with the missing words

a. Je suis **passionné** de voile   b. C'est un **endroit** idéal pour naviguer   c. Il y a **presque** toujours du vent

d. Je fais **partie** du club local   e. J'ai gagné une **course**   f. C'est mon **rêve**   g. Je dois m'**entraîner**

h. Autour du **monde**   i. Je suis **mauvais** aux sports de raquette   j. **D'habitude**, je m'entraîne le jeudi

k. En **même** temps

27. Guided English-to-French translation

a. *I am sporty (fem)*: **Je suis sportive**   b. *Since I am 5 years old*: **Depuis que j'ai cinq ans**

c. *Almost every weekend*: **Presque tous les week-ends**   d. *I do bodybuilding*: **Je fais de la musculation**

e. *Martial arts*: **Les arts martiaux**   f. *I find this boring*: **Je trouve cela ennuyeux**

g. *It's my dream*: **C'est mon rêve**   h. *Next weekend*: **Le week-end prochain**   i. *It was great*: **C'était génial**

j. *I would like to try*: **J'aimerais essayer**   k. *To do rock climbing*: **Faire de l'escalade**

28. Translate into French (sentence level translation)

a. Le week-end dernier, j'ai gagné une course. C'était génial!

b. Si je pouvais, je voudrais essayer les arts martiaux

c. J'aime l'escalade, mais c'est assez risqué

d. Je ne joue jamais au golf, c'est trop difficile

e. Le week-end prochain, j'irai au port de plaisance

f. Demain, je jouerai au badminton avec mon frère

g. Mon sport préféré, c'est l'équitation

h. Hier, j'ai joué au foot avec mes amis. C'était amusant!

i. Je suis mauvais(e) au tennis, mais je suis bon(ne) au rugby

j. Je voudrais faire de l'escalade à la montagne

29. Translate the following paragraphs into French

Une fois par semaine, je joue au volley avec mes amis. J'aime cela parce que c'est amusant et relaxant. Après le collège/l'école, parfois je fais aussi de l'athlétisme avec mon frère. Je trouve cela assez difficile.

Quand j'ai le temps, je fais du vélo avec mon père. Généralement, nous allons assez loin. C'est fatigant, mais exaltant en même temps. Je préfère les sports individuels car c'est plus compétitif.

Le week-end dernier, j'ai joué au ping-pong avec mon club, mais malheureusement j'ai perdu la compétition. J'ai aussi fait de la randonnée avec ma famille et c'était génial.

Le week-end prochain, je ferai de la musculation samedi et je jouerai au badminton avec ma sœur dimanche. Ensuite, j'irai au centre commercial avec ma petite amie.

Unit 12. Customs and festivals

1. Match up

Chez moi – *At home*   Nous fêtons – *We celebrate*   Février – *February*   Les chrétiens – *The Christians*

La mosquée – *The mosque*   Noël – *Christmas*   L'Aïd al-Fitr – *Eid al-Fitr*   La fête des mères – *Mother's Day*

Le Nouvel An – *New Year*   Les musulmans – *The Muslims*   Prier Dieu – *To pray to God*

Des cadeaux – *Gifts*   Partager – *To share*   L'église – *The church*

2. Spot and correct the 6 wrong translations

a. Chaque année: *Each year*   b. Nous fêtons: *We celebrate*   c. La fête des mères: *Mother's Day*

d. Le Nouvel An: *New Year*   e. Les juifs: The Jews   f. Le réveillon: *Christmas/NYE's dinner*

g. Un repas de fête: *A festive meal*   h. Des défilés: *Processions*   i. Je reçois: *I receive*   j. Je vois: *I see*

k. Les enfant: *Children*   l. Des cadeaux: *Gifts*   m. Des jours fériés: *Public holidays*

3. Sentence puzzle

a. Chez moi, nous fêtons le Nouvel An   b. Les chrétiens vont à l'église

c. Dans ma famille, nous fêtons l'Aïd al-Fitr   d. Il y a des feux d'artifice et des défilés

e. Je reçois des cadeaux avec mes parents   f. Les musulmans vont à la mosquée

4. Complete the table

English	Français
To their relatives	À leurs proches
To share	**Partager**
Public holidays	Des jours fériés
Gifts	**Cadeaux**
Fireworks	Des feux d'artifice
I see	Je vois
New Year	**Le Nouvel An**

5. Complete with the correct option

a. Pour prier leur **Dieu**: *To pray to their God*   b. Pendant cette **fête**: *During this festival*

c. Je **vois** ma famille: *I see my family*   d. Je reçois des **cadeaux**: *I receive gifts*

e. Des jours **fériés**: Public holidays   f. Partager un **repas** de fête: *To share a festive meal*

6. Translate into English

a. It's my favourite festival   b. I see my friends   c. We celebrate the Epiphany   d. Christians go to church

e. Muslims go to the mosque   f. Jews go to the synagogue   g. I like very much fireworks

h. I receive gifts with my parents   i. Families get together   j. To share a good time   k. I am on holidays

7. Definition game (answers in French)

a. *A spirit worshipped by believers*: **Dieu**   b. *Presents that are given*: **Cadeaux**   c. *Young persons*: **Enfants**

d. *An occasion when food is eaten*: **Repas**   e. *The first month of the year*: **Janvier**

f. *Place of worship for the Muslims*: **Mosquée**   g. *A festival celebrated on the 25th December*: **Noël**

h. *A festival involving chocolate eggs*: **Pâques**   i. *A festival to celebrate mothers*: **Fête des mères**

j. *Place of worship for the Jews*: **Synagogue**   k. *Days when people are off work*: **Jours fériés**

THE LANGUAGE GYM

8. Wordsearch: find the French translation of the words below

		M	U	S	U	L	M	A	N	S			P		P			É
	N	O	U	V	E	L	A	N					R		A			G
			I										I		R			L
	F	E	U	X	D	A	R	T	I	F	I	C	E		T			I
		P	R	O	C	H	E	S		Ê			R		A			S
									T						G			E
C	H	R	É	T	I	E	N	S		E	P	Â	Q	U	E	S		
			C	H	E	Z	M	O	I					R				

Muslims: **musulmans** fireworks: **feux d'artifice** at home: **chez moi**
church: **église** to pray: **prier** God: **Dieu**
to share: **partager** festival: **fête** Easter: **Pâques**
Christians: les **chrétiens** relatives: **proches** New Year: **Nouvel An**

9. Complete with the missing vowels

a. **Nous fêtons**: *We celebrate* b. **Nouvel An**: *New Year* c. **Chaque année**: *Each year* d. **Je reçois**: *I receive*

e. **Un repas de fête**: *A festive meal* f. **Prier Dieu**: *To pray to God* g. **Des défilés**: *Processions*

h. **Feux d'artifice**: *Fireworks*

10. Split phrases

Chez moi, nous **fêtons le Nouvel An**   Je reçois beaucoup **de cadeaux pour Noël**

La Saint-Valentin est **le quatorze février**   Les musulmans vont **à la mosquée**

À Pâques, je mange **des œufs en chocolat**   Pour le Nouvel an, **il y a des feux d'artifice**

C'est ma fête **préférée**   Je vois ma **famille et mes amis**

11. Gapped English-to-French translation

a. Pendant les fêtes **religieuses**: *During religious festivals* b. C'est ma fête **préférée**: *It's my favourite festival*

c. La fête des **pères**: *Father's Day* d. Je **vois** mes cousins: *I see my cousins*

e. J'aime les **feux** d'artifice: *I like fireworks* f. Les **chrétiens** vont à l'église: *Christians go to church*

g. Des jours **fériés**: *Public holidays* h. **Partager** un bon moment: *To share a good time*

i. Il y a des **défilés**: *There are processions* j. Je suis en **vacances**: *I am on holidays*

k. J'adore **Pâques**: *I love Easter*

12. Spot and supply the missing words

a. Je reçois beaucoup **de** cadeaux b. Pour **le** Nouvel an, il y a des feux d'artifice

c. Nous fêtons la fête **des** mères d. Les juifs vont **à** la synagogue e. Les familles **se** rencontrent

f. Dans **la** plupart des villes g. Il y a **des** concerts et des défilés h. Je suis **en** vacances pendant les jours fériés

i. C'est **ma** fête préférée j. Les amis **se** réunissent k. Les musulmans vont à **la** mosquée

13. Complete with the missing letters

a. La fête des pères b. Je vois ma famille c. Je reçois des cadeaux d. J'aime les repas de fête

e. Les chrétiens vont à l'église f. Il y a des défilés g. Les musulmans prient à la mosquée

h. Partager un bon moment

14. Phrase anagrams

a. Chez moi, nous fêtons Noël et Pâques b. Pour le Nouvel An, il y a des feux d'artifice

c. Les parents offrent des cadeaux à leurs enfants d. J'adore les jours fériés e. Il y a des concerts et des défilés

f. Les familles se rencontrent g. Les amis se réunissent pour partager un bon moment h. C'est ma fête préférée

THE LANGUAGE GYM

15. Complete with an appropriate word

a. La **fête** des Rois est en janvier   b. Chaque année, les musulmans fêtent l'**Aïd al-Fitr**

c. Les amis se réunissent pour partager un **bon** moment   d. Ces occasions spéciales sont souvent des jours **fériés**

e. Dans la plupart des villes, il y a des **défilés/concerts/feux d'artifice**

f. À **Pâques**, je mange toujours des œufs en chocolat   g. J'adore regarder les **feux** d'artifice au Nouvel An

h. J'adore Noël, c'est ma **fête** préférée   i. Je **reçois** des cadeaux avec mes parents

j. Les gens offrent des cadeaux à leurs **enfants/proches/amis**   k. C'est ma période préférée de l'**année**

l. Les juifs prient à la **synagogue**

16. Guided translation

a. *Each year*: **Chaque année**   b. *The Epiphany*: **La fête des Rois**   c. *Mother's Day:* **La fête des mères**

d. *A good time*: **Un bon moment**   e. *Fireworks*: **Des feux d'artifice**

f. *To pray to their God*: **Pour prier leur Dieu**   g. *A festive meal*: **Un repas de fête**

h. *The Muslims*: **Les musulmans**   i. *At home*: **Chez moi**   j. *People offer*: **Les gens offrent**

k. *Friends get together*: **Les amis se réunissent**   l. *Families meet*: **Les familles se rencontrent**

17. Find the French match in the text in paragraph 1

a. *Today*: **Aujourd'hui**   b. *Festivals*: **Fêtes**   c. *At home*: **Chez moi**   d. *We celebrate*: **Nous fêtons**

e. *Christmas*: **Noël**   f. *This*: **Cette**   g. *I am on holidays*: **Je suis en vacances**   h. *I see*: **Je vois**

i. *Good*: **Bon**   j. *Together*: **Ensemble**

18. Complete the translation of paragraph 2

During **this** religious **festival**, we go to midnight **mass** as a family, just after Christmas Eve **dinner**. It's the **only** time of the year when I **go** to **church** and I must **say** that **it's** always a **beautiful** ceremony. Of course, I also **love** Christmas because each **year**, I decorate the Christmas **tree** with my **sister**. There are **garlands/tinsels** and **pretty** lights everywhere. In addition, I receive **gifts** from my parents, my godfather and my **godmother**.

19. Spot and supply the <u>ten</u> missing words in this wrong version of paragraph 3

Juste **une** semaine après Noël, il y **a** le Nouvel An le 31 décembre. Cette fois-ci, je fête **cela** avec mes amis. La plupart **du** temps c'est chez l'un **d'entre** nous. Chacun apporte quelque chose **à** manger et à boire et nous écoutons **de** la musique et nous dansons. À minuit, tout **le** monde se souhaite "bonne année" et ensuite **on** continue **à** faire la fête jusqu'à tard dans la nuit.

20. Translate into English the words and phrases below taken from paragraph 3

a. *One week after*: **Une semaine après**   b. *This time*: **Cette fois-ci**   c. *I celebrate this*: **Je fête cela**

d. *Most of the time*: **La plupart du temps**   e. *Each one brings something*: **Chacun apporte quelque chose**

f. *We dance*: **Nous dansons**   g. *Everyone wishes one another*: **Tout le monde se souhaite**

21. Tick the 5 items in the list below which are in the text and cross the 5 which aren't

a. Yesterday **X**   b. Today **√**   c. Until **√**   d. Tomorrow **X**   e. Godfather **√**   f. Mosque **X**

g. Public holidays **X**   h. Midnight **√**   i. Month **X**   j. Christmas tree **√**

22. True (T), False (F) or Not mentioned (NM)

a. Benoît is Christian **T**   b. His girlfriend is Muslim **T**   c. Benoît has two siblings **NM**

d. Easter is his favourite festival **F**   e. He trains twice a week **T**   f. He sees all his relatives for Christmas **T**

g. He goes to church during religious festivals **T**   h. According to the text, fasting is easy during Ramadan **F**

i. You can only eat during the daytime for Ramadan **F**   j. He is going to celebrate Valentine's Day this year **T**

k. He is going to buy jewellery for his girlfriend **F**

23. Find the French equivalent in the text

a. *New Year's Day*: **Le jour de l'An**   b. *I don't have school*: **Je n'ai pas école**

c. *I see all my relatives*: **Je vois tous mes proches**   d. *I go to mass at church*: **Je vais à la messe à l'église**

e. *They celebrate*: **Ils fêtent**   f. *My girlfriend*: **Ma petite amie**   g. *Mainly*: **Principalement**

h. *At the end of the month*: **À la fin du mois**   i. *Devotion*: **Dévouement**

j. *Until sunset*: **Jusqu'au coucher du soleil**   k. *Every evening*: **Tous les soirs**

l. *To offer flowers*: **Offrir des fleurs**

24. Faulty translation – correct the <u>eight</u> errors in the translation of paragraph 4 below

This year, my **girlfriend** and I, we will celebrate together Valentine's Day on the 14th **February**. Valentine's Day is the festival for lovers everywhere in the **world**. I am going to **offer** her some **flowers** and I am going to go to the restaurant with her. **Afterwards**, we will go to the cinema. It will be very **romantic**.

25. Word hunt – find in the text a word for each of the definitions below and translate it into English

a. The other expression for "Nouvel An": **Jour de l'An**   b. The word for "*Christmas/NYE's dinner*": **Réveillon**

c. The male version of "marraine": **Parrain**   d. The French word for "*mass*": **Messe**

e. "*Sunrise*" in French: **Lever du jour**   f. The word for "*fasting*": **Jeûne**

g. The word for "*devotion*": **Dévouement**

26. Complete with the missing words

a. En **compagnie** de mes amis   b. Je reçois beaucoup de **cadeaux**   c. Je vais à la **messe** à l'**église**

d. Les musulmans font le **jeûne**   e. Du **lever** du **jour**   f. Jusqu'au **coucher** du **soleil**   g. Nous fêterons **ensemble**

h. **Partout** dans le monde   i. **Offrir** des fleurs   j. Nous **irons** au cinéma   k. Ce **sera** très romantique

27. Guided English-to-French translation

a. *I am going to talk about*: **Je vais parler de**   b. *I see all my family*: **Je vois toute ma famille**

c. *At my grandparents' place*: **Chez mes grands-parents**   d. *I go to mass*: **Je vais à la messe**

e. *My godfather*: **Mon parrain**   f. *My godmother*: **Ma marraine**   g. *We get together*: **Nous nous réunissons**

h. *It's the only time*: **C'est la seule fois**   i. *To offer flowers*: **Offrir des fleurs**

j. *Everywhere in the world*: **Partout dans le monde**   k. *Until sunset*: **Jusqu'au coucher du soleil**

28. Translate into French (sentence level translation)

a. Je vois tous mes proches à Noël   b. Chacun apporte quelque chose à manger

c. Il y a toujours beaucoup de feux d'artifice   d. C'est la fête des amoureux   e. Ce sera très romantique

f. Nous irons au cinéma   g. Je vais à la messe à l'église   h. Du lever du jour jusqu'au coucher du soleil

i. Je vais aller au restaurant   j. Dans la plupart des villes

29. Translate the following paragraphs into French

Dans ma famille, nous fêtons principalement Noël et Pâques. Noël est ma fête préférée parce que je suis en vacances, et je vois tous mes proches. Généralement, je vais à la messe et puis nous avons un repas de fête.

Chaque année, je reçois des cadeaux avec mes parents et ma marraine, c'est génial! L'année dernière, je suis allé(e) au marché de Noël dans ma ville et j'ai acheté des chocolats pour mes grands-parents.

J'aime aussi le Nouvel An, car cette fois-ci je vois mes amis et c'est amusant. La plupart du temps, il y a des concerts en centre-ville et puis des feux d'artifice à minuit.

En février, ma petite amie et moi, nous fêterons la Saint-Valentin ensemble. Je vais lui offrir des fleurs et nous irons au cinéma. Ce sera romantique.

THE LANGUAGE GYM

Printed in Great Britain
by Amazon

38158748R00037